The Emasculation of America

How Russia's Long War Against the American Male

Is Destroying the Nation from Within

Richard Lowe
The Writing King

Enemies of You Series

https://masterofworlds.com/enemies-of-you

The Emasculation of America: How Russia's Long War Against the American Male Is Destroying the Nation from Within

A Note to the Reader

This book is a national security argument. It is not an attack on any individual's personal philosophy, lifestyle, political beliefs, or choices about how to live.

The ideological framework this book examines is analyzed as a strategic delivery mechanism, a set of ideas that were seeded, amplified, and institutionalized in ways that served the interests of foreign adversaries and produced measurable damage to American national capacity. That analysis is about the framework's origins, its institutional deployment, and its strategic effects. It is not a judgment on any person who holds beliefs shaped by that framework, any more than documenting the effects of a propaganda operation is a judgment on the people the propaganda reached.

People arrive at their beliefs through their education, their experiences, their relationships, and the culture around them. Most people who hold the views this book examines hold them sincerely, arrived at them honestly, and are trying to make the world better as they understand it. This book does not dispute their sincerity. It disputes the origins and effects of the framework they are working within, and it documents what the evidence shows about who built that framework, how it was delivered, and who benefits from its persistence.

If your personal philosophy includes commitments to fairness, to the dignity of all people, to honest examination of how power operates in society, this book is not arguing against those commitments. It is arguing that the specific framework examined here does not reliably produce those outcomes, and that understanding where it came from changes what you can expect it to produce.

This book is for anyone who wants to understand what happened to the men around them and why. It is for men who felt the ground shift under them and never got a clear account of what produced the shift. It is for women who are watching men they care about check out and cannot find an explanation that fits. It is for parents trying to understand what the educational system is doing to their sons. It is for citizens who believe that America is worth defending and who want to understand what has been done to the people who defend it.

It is not for people who want to be told that one sex is superior to the other, that the answer to the problems documented here is hostility toward women, or that the men who have been damaged by this operation are therefore absolved of responsibility for their own choices and their own lives. The operation is real. The damage is real. Neither is an excuse. They are an explanation that points toward a response, and the response this book recommends has nothing to do with hostility and everything to do with building.

Read it for what it is: a documented account of a strategic operation, its mechanisms, its damage, and what the evidence suggests about how to respond to it. Take what is useful. Examine what is disputed. Check the primary sources. The argument either holds up to that examination or it does not.

One final statement before you begin. The United States has real enemies. Those enemies do not limit themselves to military attack vectors. They study American society for vulnerabilities, identify the pressure points that will produce the most damage at the least cost, and apply sustained institutional effort to exploiting those pressure points over years and decades. This is not a theory. It is the documented operational history of Soviet active measures, continued by Russia through its successor intelligence services, and adopted and refined by China into something more sophisticated than the original. The vector this book documents (the systematic targeting of American masculinity as a mechanism for degrading American national capacity) is one of the most successful non-military attacks ever conducted against this country. It is still running. The men it targeted are in the data. The enemies who designed it are named in the chapters that follow. Read this as what it is: a national security document about an attack that most Americans do not know is happening to them.

Table of Contents

See books by Richard Lowe at

https://masterofworlds.com

Get free publishing insights and industry updates at

https://thewritingking.substack.com

For ghostwriting and book coaching services see

https://thewritingking.com

Enemies of You Series

https://masterofworlds.com/enemies-of-you

The Death of Thinking
The Enslavement of Humanity

The Birth of the Augmented Human
The Freeing of Humanity

Turn Off The TV, Get Off Your Ass, and Do Something

Stuck in the Middle
Wars, Weapons, and the Forces That Will Shape the Next Thirty Years

The Enshittification of America
How Private Equity Destroyed the Things We Love

The Emasculation of America
How Russia's Long War Against the American Male Is Destroying the Nation From Within

The Villainization of America

———

See the full series description at the back of this book.

All books available at masterofworlds.com

Preface

I did not set out to write a book about the emasculation of America. I set out to understand what I was watching on YouTube.

For months I had been falling down the rabbit hole of videos documenting something that did not have a clean name yet but was impossible to miss once you started looking. Men and women who could not stand each other. Not in the usual way people who disagree argue, with some heat and some humor and the assumption that the other person is still a reasonable human being. Something colder and more absolute than that. Men who had given up on women entirely. Women who had concluded that men were the problem and acted accordingly. Both sides producing content at industrial scale, each video feeding an audience that had already decided, and comment sections full of people who sounded like they were preparing for a war nobody had formally declared.

I watched enough of it to know it was not fringe. The view counts were too high. The audiences were too large and too young. Something was happening to the relationship between men and women in America at a scale that the mainstream conversation was not tracking, or was tracking badly, or was actively making worse.

My first instinct was that this was a cultural problem. A social media problem. Maybe a generational problem. Something organic that had grown out of legitimate grievances on both sides and been amplified by algorithms that profit from conflict. That instinct was not wrong. It was just incomplete.

The further I looked, the more a different picture emerged. The divide I was watching on YouTube did not start on YouTube. The ideology that had declared traditional masculinity a disease did not arise spontaneously from American soil. The institutions that now treat normal male behavior as a problem to be corrected did not arrive at that position through independent reasoning. There was a thread running through all of it, back through decades of academic capture and social media manipulation and foreign influence operations, back to a decision made by Soviet strategic planners in the middle of the last century.

The decision was simple. You cannot beat America in a straight fight. You cannot outspend it, outproduce it, or outlast it on a conventional battlefield. So you do not fight it conventionally. You fight its culture. You fight its confidence. You fight the men who would defend it by convincing them, and the women around them, that the traits that made those men worth defending anything are the traits that make them dangerous.

That operation has been running for sixty years. This book is the account of how it worked, what it produced, and what it is still producing right now.

I want to be clear about what this book is and what it is not. It is not a culture war book. It does not take sides in the argument between men who feel wronged and women who feel threatened. It does not blame women for what happened and it does not excuse men for their part in it. It is a national security argument. The question it asks is not who is right in the conflict playing out on YouTube. The question it asks is who benefits from that conflict existing at the scale it does, and how it got there.

The answers are documented. Declassified. On the record in Senate Intelligence Committee reports and KGB defector testimony and academic research that has been sitting in plain sight for decades waiting for someone to connect it to what is happening right now on the screens in your pocket.

A word about sources. Every major claim in this book is sourced. The Mitrokhin Archive. The Senate Intelligence Committee reports on Russian active measures. The Bezmenov interviews, which are on YouTube and have been since 2013 and which most people who should have watched them have not. The peer-reviewed research on hormonal contraceptives and behavior. The educational achievement data. The military recruitment numbers. The TikTok content research. The academic cult identification criteria that apply to the ideology this book examines with a precision that should make everyone uncomfortable.

This book will generate blowback. I know that going in and I do not care. I am getting older, I prefer my own company, and I stopped worrying about what people think of my conclusions around the same time I started being more interested in whether those conclusions were true. The blowback will come from people who have not read it carefully and people who have read it carefully and do not like where the argument goes. Both groups are welcome to their response. The documentation will still be there.

What I watched on YouTube was real. The men checking out are real. The women who cannot find men worth choosing are real. The boys falling behind in school are real. The military that cannot find qualified recruits is real. The birth rate below replacement is real. The testosterone decline is real. None of it happened by accident and none of it is going to fix itself.

This book is the account of why. What you do with that account is up to you.

Introduction: The Warning Nobody Heard

In 1984, a man named Yuri Bezmenov sat down in front of a camera in Los Angeles and explained, in calm and careful detail, exactly what was being done to America.

Bezmenov was a KGB defector. He had spent years working for Soviet intelligence, running active measures operations in India before defecting to the West in 1970. By 1984 he had been trying for over a decade to get anyone in a position of authority to listen to what he knew. He gave lectures. He wrote reports. He did interviews. The interview he gave that year to G. Edward Griffin ran for over an hour and covered the entire Soviet strategy for defeating the United States without firing a shot.

Nobody listened.

That sentence requires some precision. It is not that nobody heard him. The interview was conducted and distributed. His lectures were given to real audiences. His reports went to real people. The more accurate statement is that the people in positions to act on what he was saying looked at his description of what was being done to America and concluded, for reasons that seemed reasonable at the time, that the threat he was describing was not real enough or not urgent enough to require the kind of response he was calling for. They were wrong. The record is now available to anyone. Bezmenov described a four-stage operation in 1984. You can check his description against what happened in the forty years that followed. The match is not approximate. It is precise. A KGB defector sat on camera in Los Angeles and told America exactly what was being done to it, in operational detail, and the country did not listen, and the operation continued, and the results are in the data chapters of this book.

The interview sat in obscurity for decades. It resurfaced on YouTube around 2013 and has been watched millions of times since then, mostly by people who recognized in it a description of something they were already watching happen. If you have not seen it, you should watch it before you read this book. Not because everything Bezmenov said was correct or because Soviet defectors are infallible sources, but because the degree to which his 1984 description matches what happened in the forty years that followed is something you need to experience rather than just read about.

What Bezmenov described was a four-stage process the Soviets called ideological subversion. The first stage was demoralization, and he said it took fifteen to twenty years to complete because that was how long it took to educate one generation of students. You got inside the universities. You put your people in the faculty. You shaped what the next generation of teachers, journalists, politicians, and corporate executives believed before they were old enough to question it. By the time they were running the institutions, they would carry the ideology with them without knowing where it came from or recognizing it as foreign.

The second stage was destabilization. Two to five years of targeting the economy, the military structure, and foreign relations. The third stage was crisis, a period of rapid collapse in existing institutions. The fourth stage was normalization, the point at which the new reality was accepted as permanent and nobody could remember clearly what it had been like before.

Bezmenov was describing the Soviet strategy as of 1984. The Soviet Union collapsed seven years later. The strategy did not collapse with it.

Russia inherited the KGB's active measures apparatus along with everything else. The Internet Research Agency, which the Senate Intelligence Committee documented in exhaustive detail in 2019, was running the same playbook that Bezmenov had described, updated for social media, targeted with far more precision than the Soviets ever managed, and funded at a level that produced results at industrial scale. The goal had not changed. The delivery mechanism had gotten better.

China watched and learned and then built something more ambitious. Where Russia used social media to amplify existing divisions, China built the platform. TikTok is not a neutral technology company that happens to be owned by a Chinese firm. It is a content delivery system that serves Chinese youth material promoting discipline, achievement, and national pride, and serves American youth material designed to maximize confusion, conflict, and institutional distrust. This is documented. Researchers have run the comparison. The algorithm is not the same algorithm in both countries. The difference is a strategic choice.

This book covers the full operation: the Soviet origins, the academic delivery mechanism, the social media acceleration, the Chinese amplification, and the biological dimension that ran alongside all of it in a way that nobody planned but that served the operation's goals regardless. It covers what the operation produced in measurable terms: the educational collapse among boys, the military recruitment crisis, the testosterone decline, the birth rate, the marriage rate, the workforce participation numbers, the suicide rate. It covers who benefits from all of it and what that comparison looks like when you put American numbers next to Russian and Chinese numbers in the same categories.

One chapter deserves special mention before you reach it. The chapter on the cult applies academic cult identification criteria to the ideology that has been delivered through this operation. Twelve criteria developed by researchers who study destructive groups, applied one by one to the belief system that now governs university campuses, HR departments, corporate training programs, and increasingly the K-12 classroom. The match is close enough to be uncomfortable regardless of where you sit politically. Read it carefully. The criteria are not partisan.

They describe a structure. The structure is either present or it is not.

This book is not about gender. It is not about feminism or the men's rights movement or any of the proxy arguments that keep the real argument from being had. It is about a nation that has been targeted by its enemies through a specific vector, has taken real damage from that targeting, and has not yet named what was done to it clearly enough to mount a serious response.

Bezmenov tried to name it in 1984. He sat on camera in Los Angeles and said, calmly, that the demoralization was already complete. That the people who had been exposed to it could not be reasoned out of it because their capacity to evaluate evidence had been damaged by the process itself. That the only thing that could reverse it was a significant change in conditions, something that made the cost of the ideology visible in terms that people could not dismiss.

He was talking about 1984. Look at where we are now and consider what he would say about the forty years that followed.

This book is the account of those forty years. What was done. How it was done. What it cost. And what the men and communities that refused to go along with it look like, because they exist, and their existence is the only honest basis for optimism this book can offer.

Bezmenov said nobody would listen until it was almost too late.

A note on language before you read further. This book uses the word "operation" to describe two specific things: the Soviet active measures programs documented in the Mitrokhin Archive and the Senate Intelligence Committee reports, and the Russian Internet Research Agency campaigns that followed them. These were actual operations, organized, funded, directed, and executed with strategic intent. When this book uses that word, it means those things.

The other forces documented here, the Frankfurt School's intellectual influence, the hormonal changes produced by contraceptives and environmental estrogens, the algorithmic dynamics of social media platforms, the domestic attention economy, were not coordinated with the Soviet and Russian programs. They were not directed by the same actors or toward the same explicit goals. What they share is convergence: independent forces that moved in the same direction and compounded each other's effects. This book uses "the convergence" or "the combined effect" when describing these uncoordinated forces, and reserves "operation" for what was an operation. The distinction matters and the book means it.

We are at almost.

Part One: The Weapon

You don't defeat the most powerful nation on earth with missiles.

You defeat it with ideas.

Chapter 1: The Decision

I want to start with a number, because it is the number that convinced me this book needed to exist.

The United States Army missed its recruiting goal by fifteen thousand soldiers in 2022. Seven million prime-age American men have permanently exited the labor force. Male testosterone levels have declined by roughly one percent per year for several decades. Boys are failing in school at rates that have no historical precedent. The birth rate is below replacement. The suicide rate among men is four times the rate among women and rising. None of this happened by accident. None of it is the inevitable product of modernization or social progress. It is the measurable outcome of a decision made by a group of men in Moscow in the early 1950s, accelerated by their successors, and now being completed by Beijing with tools the original architects could not have imagined.

In the early 1950s, a group of men sitting in Moscow ran a calculation.

The calculation was not complicated. The United States had emerged from World War II as the most powerful nation in human history. Its industrial base was intact and expanding while Europe lay in rubble. Its military had demonstrated the capacity to project force anywhere on earth and had ended the war with a weapon that nothing in existence could counter. Its economy was producing wealth at a scale the Soviet Union could not match and would not match in the foreseeable future. Its population was educated, optimistic, and producing children at a rate that would sustain that advantage for generations.

A direct military confrontation with America would end the Soviet Union. That was the conclusion. Not might end it. Would end it. The men running the calculation were not stupid, and they did not arrive at a different answer no matter how many times they ran the numbers.

So they asked a different question. If you cannot fight something directly, what do you fight instead?

The answer they arrived at was the culture.

The Logic of Indirect Attack

The Soviet strategic doctrine that emerged from this period was not invented from nothing. It drew on a long tradition of what Russian intelligence called "active measures", operations designed to shape the enemy's political environment rather than defeat his military. The concept predated the Soviet Union. The Tsarist secret police, the Okhrana, had run influence operations against political enemies for decades. The Bolsheviks refined the approach after 1917 and built an institutional infrastructure for it that the KGB inherited and expanded.

What changed in the 1950s was the scale of the ambition. Previous active measures operations had targeted specific political opponents or specific elections. What the Soviet planners were now considering was something larger: the systematic corruption of an entire civilization's confidence in itself.

The logic was simple. A nation that believes in itself is hard to subvert. It resists foreign influence because it has its own framework for evaluating information and its own reasons for defending its institutions. A nation that has been taught to doubt itself, to see its own history as a source of shame rather than pride, to view its traditions as oppression rather than inheritance, is a nation that has lost its immune system. It cannot mount a coherent defense against ideas it has already been conditioned to accept.

The target they chose was not the government. Governments could be pressured, negotiated with, or isolated. The target was the next generation, the generation that would be educated in American universities between roughly 1960 and 1985, the generation that would then spend the following three decades running American media, education, corporations, and cultural institutions.

Get inside the universities. Shape what that generation believed. Wait.

The investment required was modest. The return, if the operation worked, would be permanent.

What the Mitrokhin Archive Tells Us

In 1992, a retired KGB archivist named Vasili Mitrokhin walked into the British Embassy in Riga, Latvia, carrying something extraordinary. For twelve years, he had been hand-copying classified KGB operational files. He had hidden the copies under the floorboards of his dacha outside Moscow. He now wanted to bring them to the West.

The British Secret Intelligence Service spent the next several years extracting Mitrokhin and his archive from the former Soviet Union. What he brought out was the most complete record of KGB foreign operations ever made available to Western intelligence agencies. It documented operations in over a hundred countries across four decades. It named agents, described methods, and specified targets with the kind of operational detail that intelligence agencies normally never see.

What the archive confirmed was what Western intelligence had suspected for years about Soviet active measures. The KGB had funded and directed operations designed to amplify radical movements in the United States throughout the 1960s and 1970s. This did not mean the movements were invented by Moscow. They were not. The civil rights movement, the anti-war movement, the women's liberation movement, all of these arose from genuine American grievances and genuine American conditions. What the KGB did was identify which of these movements could be amplified to produce maximum social division, and then amplify them.

That distinction matters and it is easy to miss. The Soviet operation was not primarily about creating conflict. It was about preventing resolution. A society that argues, examines its grievances, and reforms itself emerges stronger. A society that argues without resolution, that has its wounds kept open and its divisions widened, exhausts itself. The KGB understood the difference and worked the second outcome.

Specific operations documented in the Mitrokhin Archive included funding for radical publications, support for activist organizations that promoted the most divisive possible framing of American social conflicts, and disinformation campaigns designed to deepen mistrust between different groups within American society. The archive documented KGB agent networks inside American universities, inside media organizations, and inside political movements on both the left and the right.

The archive also documented something that received less attention than it deserved when the material was published in the late 1990s. Soviet active measures had targeted the relationship between American men and women. Operations designed to deepen conflict between the sexes, to promote the idea that American masculinity was inherently dangerous, and to seed the intellectual frameworks that would eventually produce the academic gender studies programs that trained the next generation of teachers, journalists, and HR professionals. This targeting is not documented in a single explicit operational file, the Archive does not work that way. It emerges from the pattern of documented operations: which movements received funding, which framings were amplified, which academic networks received support, and how the aggregate of those decisions consistently pushed in the same direction. The pattern is the documentation.

This was not an accident of timing. It was a strategic priority.

This is the point at which critics will object that correlation between Soviet funding and cultural change does not establish Soviet causation. The objection is partly correct and should be stated clearly. The Soviet contribution to what this book documents was amplification, not creation. The Frankfurt School existed and was spreading independently. The civil rights movement, the anti-war movement, the women's liberation movement, all arose from genuine American conditions. The academic gender studies apparatus developed through the work of genuine American scholars pursuing genuine intellectual programs. None of this required Soviet direction. What the active measures operation did was identify the elements already moving in the strategically useful direction and accelerate them, funding the most divisive framings, amplifying the most extreme voices, keeping wounds open that American institutions might otherwise have closed. The ideology is American in origin. The systematic effort to prevent its resolution is not.

Why Masculinity Was the Target

The Soviet planners who designed the cultural subversion operation understood something that most of their American counterparts did not think about in strategic terms: masculine culture is a civilization's immune system.

This is not a romantic idea. It is a structural one. Every human society that has survived long enough to leave a historical record developed mechanisms for channeling male energy toward the defense and maintenance of that society. The specifics varied enormously across cultures and across time. The common thread was that men were expected to provide, protect, and if necessary fight, and that the culture around them reinforced those expectations through institutions, rituals, and social rewards.

A culture that maintains that framework produces men who are willing to defend it. A culture that dismantles that framework produces men who have no particular stake in its survival. The military implication is direct and the Soviet planners saw it clearly. An America whose men did not believe in American masculinity would be an America that could not field an effective military, could not maintain the civic participation that democratic governance requires, and could not produce the next generation of children that any civilization needs to survive.

You did not need to defeat the American military. You needed to produce conditions in which the American military could not recruit, could not retain, and could not maintain the culture of martial excellence that made it dangerous. You needed to produce conditions in which American men, the young men who would fill the ranks of that military, had been taught that the traits that made them good soldiers (competitiveness, aggression, physical courage, willingness to use force in defense of something larger than themselves) were pathological rather than admirable.

The operation that would produce those conditions was not a single program with a single director. It was a set of overlapping efforts, some run directly by Soviet intelligence, some run by ideologically aligned actors who needed no direction, some the product of genuine American intellectual movements that happened to serve Soviet strategic interests without any coordination at all. The Soviets did not need to control every element. They needed to identify the elements that were moving in the right direction and amplify them.

Herbert Marcuse did not work for the KGB. The Frankfurt School theorists who developed the critical theory that became the intellectual foundation of gender studies, critical race theory, and the broader ideological framework now institutionalized in American universities were not Soviet agents. They were genuine Marxist intellectuals who arrived in America as refugees from Nazi Germany and spent the rest of their careers developing a theory of cultural revolution that happened to align almost perfectly with what Soviet active measures were trying to produce.

The Soviets did not create the Frankfurt School. They did not need to. They needed only to recognize what it was producing and support the institutions that were spreading it.

The Sixty-Year Timeline

The operation that Bezmenov described in 1984 was already thirty years old when he sat down to describe it. The demoralization phase, the fifteen to twenty years of university capture that he identified as the foundation of everything else, had begun in the early 1960s. By 1984, the first generation of students educated under those conditions was already running significant portions of American media, academia, and culture.

By the time the Soviet Union collapsed in 1991, the operation had produced results that could not be undone simply because its original sponsor was gone. The ideology that had been seeded in American universities was self-replicating. The professors trained in Frankfurt School critical theory trained the next generation of professors. The journalists educated in institutions where that theory was dominant brought its assumptions into newsrooms. The HR professionals who had absorbed its frameworks in college brought them into corporations. The teachers who had learned it in education schools brought it into classrooms.

The Soviet Union died. The operation continued under its own momentum.

Russia understood this. The KGB's successor organizations, the FSB and the GRU, did not abandon active measures when the Soviet Union collapsed. They adapted them. The Internet Research Agency, which began serious operations around 2014 and was documented in detail by the Senate Intelligence Committee in 2019, was running the same fundamental playbook that the KGB had run, updated for the social media environment that had not existed when Bezmenov gave his 1984 interview.

Racial conflict, political polarization, and gender relations were all targeted at once by IRA operations against American social cohesion. Senate Intelligence Committee findings established that IRA accounts ran operations on both sides of every major social divide, not to promote any particular ideology but to maximize the conflict between existing American communities. They created Facebook groups for Black Lives Matter and for groups opposing Black Lives Matter. They created accounts promoting feminist content and accounts promoting men's rights content. The goal was not to move American opinion in any particular direction. The goal was to ensure that Americans on opposite sides of every divide could not hear each other.

That gender conflict, the one that produced the YouTube rabbit hole I described in the preface did not start with Russian bots. The genuine grievances that men and women in America have developed toward each other over the past sixty years are real and they arose from real conditions. But the scale of the conflict, the speed at which reasonable disagreement became total mutual contempt, the degree to which every attempt at conversation across the divide became a flashpoint, that was amplified. Deliberately, professionally, and with a clear strategic purpose.

The Decision and Its Consequences

The men who made the decision in Moscow in the early 1950s are long dead. The Soviet Union they served is gone. The

Cold War that framed their calculations ended more than thirty years ago. None of this matters to the operation they set in motion, because the operation they set in motion was not designed to end. It was designed to become self-sustaining.

A factory can be closed. An ideology planted in a university and allowed to propagate through three generations of students cannot be closed. It can only be countered, which requires first naming it clearly enough to counter it.

This chapter is the naming.

The chapters that follow are the documentation: how the ideology was delivered through academic institutions, how it was structured to function as a cult, how the biological dimension ran alongside the cultural one, how social media became the acceleration mechanism, and how China adopted and improved on the Russian model with a precision that the original architects would have admired.

The decision made in Moscow seventy years ago produced consequences that are measurable in American data today. The boys falling behind in school, the men checking out of the workforce, the military that cannot find recruits, the birth rate below replacement, the testosterone levels in documented decline across five consecutive decades, these are not the inevitable products of social progress. They are the measurable outcomes of a strategic operation that targeted them.

Understanding that changes what the problem is. A cultural drift can be waited out or gradually reversed. A strategic operation requires a strategic response.

The first step in any strategic response is knowing what you are responding to.

Now you know.

Chapter 2: The Frankfurt School Pipeline

When I trace the ideology documented in this book back to its origins, I end up in Frankfurt, Germany, in 1923.

In 1923, a group of Marxist intellectuals in Frankfurt, Germany founded an institute they called the Institut für Sozialforschung, the Institute for Social Research. Their problem was a practical one. The Marxist revolution that was supposed to sweep the industrial West after World War One had not arrived. The German working class had not risen. The revolution had happened in Russia, a pre-industrial agrarian society that Marx himself would not have predicted as the birthplace of communism. Something had gone wrong with the theory, and the men at the Frankfurt Institute wanted to understand what.

Their answer, developed over the following decade, was that the problem was culture. The working class had not risen because capitalism had not just exploited workers economically. It had colonized their minds. Popular culture, mass media, religion, the family structure, the entire apparatus of what they called the "culture industry" had produced workers who identified with the system that exploited them rather than with the class interest that should have driven them to overthrow it. You could not have a political revolution without first having a cultural revolution. The superstructure had to be dismantled before the base could be changed.

This was not a fringe position. It was a rigorous intellectual program developed by serious thinkers working at the intersection of Marxist theory, Freudian psychology, and German idealist philosophy. The names associated with it (Max Horkheimer, Theodor Adorno, Erich Fromm, Herbert Marcuse, Walter Benjamin) became foundational figures in twentieth-century social theory. Their work was sophisticated, challenging, and genuinely influential on serious academic discourse across multiple disciplines.

It was also a blueprint for exactly the kind of cultural subversion that Soviet active measures were trying to produce, developed independently, by people with no loyalty to Moscow, arriving at conclusions that served Soviet strategic interests without any coordination at all.

When Hitler came to power in 1933, the Frankfurt School relocated. Most of its members were Jewish and most were Marxists. Germany was no longer safe for either. The Institute moved first to Geneva, then to New York, where it affiliated with Columbia University. The men who had developed a theory of cultural revolution in Weimar Germany were now inside one of the most prestigious academic institutions in the United States, with access to American graduate students, American publishing houses, and the American intellectual mainstream.

They stayed.

I should say plainly what I cannot prove. I cannot draw a straight line from a decision made in Moscow to the specific content that appeared in a specific American university classroom. The archive documents intent, funding, and direction. It does not document every link in the chain. What I can document is the pattern, the timing, the documented operations, and the fact that the outcomes served Soviet strategic interests. Whether that constitutes causation or remarkably convenient coincidence is a judgment call I am making, and I want the reader to know I am making it.

A necessary clarification before proceeding. The Frankfurt School was not a monolithic movement with a unified program. Its first generation (Horkheimer, Adorno, Benjamin) were rigorous and often pessimistic thinkers who would have rejected much of what their intellectual descendants built on their foundations. Adorno in particular was deeply skeptical of mass political movements and would likely have been appalled by the identity politics framework that later academics developed from critical theory. The pipeline this chapter documents is not a straight line from 1923 to the present. It is a selective inheritance, specific threads pulled from a complex body of work, amplified by subsequent generations, and deployed in institutional settings in ways the original theorists did not intend and would not all have endorsed. Acknowledging that complexity does not weaken the pipeline argument. It makes it more precise. The question is not whether Horkheimer would have approved of mandatory diversity training. The question is which threads were selected, why those threads rather than others, and who benefited from the selection.

Marcuse and the Pivot to Culture

Of all the Frankfurt School thinkers, Herbert Marcuse had the most direct and documented influence on the American counterculture of the 1960s and on the academic framework that followed it. His 1955 book Eros and Civilization applied Freudian theory to Marxist politics and argued that sexual liberation was inseparable from political liberation. His 1964 One-Dimensional Man argued that advanced industrial society had produced a form of totalitarianism more insidious than anything in Soviet Russia because it operated through comfort and consumption rather than through force, producing people who could not even conceive of alternatives to the system they lived in.

These were not simple ideas and they did not produce simple results. But they gave the student movements of the 1960s an intellectual framework that transformed what might have remained localized political protests into something with genuine theoretical ambitions. The students who read Marcuse were not just opposing the Vietnam War. They were, in their own understanding, engaged in the dismantling of an entire civilization's value system.

Marcuse's concept of repressive tolerance was the most directly consequential. Published in 1965 as part of a collection called A Critique of Pure Tolerance, it argued that the liberal tradition of tolerating all viewpoints was itself a form of repression when it treated conservative and revolutionary ideas as equally deserving of consideration. True tolerance, Marcuse argued, required intolerance of viewpoints that served the interests of oppression. The left had the obligation to suppress ideas it identified as reactionary.

Read that again slowly. A leading intellectual at a major American university published a philosophical argument that suppressing conservative ideas was not a violation of tolerance but a fulfillment of it. In 1965. And then spent the next decade watching those ideas move from academic journals into student activism into university policy into the broader culture.

If you want to understand where campus speech codes came from, where the logic of no-platforming originated, where the argument that some ideas are too dangerous to debate was first developed into a coherent philosophical position, it came from Herbert Marcuse at the University of California San Diego, publishing in respected academic presses, cited by serious scholars, incorporated into the curriculum of the universities that trained the next generation of American academics.

The Long March

The phrase "long march through the institutions" is commonly attributed to Mao Zedong but was coined by the German student activist Rudi Dutschke in 1967. Dutschke was describing a strategy for radical political change that abandoned the revolutionary seizure of state power in favor of something slower and more thorough: the systematic placement of ideologically aligned people inside every significant cultural institution until those institutions reflected the ideology rather than opposing it.

Universities first. Then schools of education, because the people who trained the next generation of teachers were more important than any individual teacher. Then journalism schools. Then law schools. Then the professional associations that certified practitioners in each field and set the standards that defined acceptable practice.

The strategy did not require coordination. It required only shared assumptions. A generation of students educated in Frankfurt School critical theory did not need to be organized into cells or given instructions. They simply carried their education with them into the institutions they entered, hired people who shared their assumptions when they gained the power to hire, and gradually transformed the institutional culture from inside.

The timeline Bezmenov described (fifteen to twenty years per generation, the demoralization phase taking one educational cycle to complete) is exactly what you see when you trace the Frankfurt School's influence through American academia. The first generation of American students seriously exposed to critical theory in significant numbers graduated in the late 1960s and early 1970s. They entered graduate programs, journalism, law, and education in the 1970s. They were in positions of institutional influence by the 1980s. They were training the next generation of academics, journalists, lawyers, and teachers by the 1990s. The generation they trained was running significant portions of American cultural institutions by 2000 and had near-total dominance of certain fields by 2010.

Seventy years from a group of refugee intellectuals affiliating with Columbia University to mandatory diversity training in Fortune 500 corporations. One generation at a time, each one moving the baseline further in the same direction, each one training the next from within institutions that the previous generation had already transformed.

What Critical Theory Did to Masculinity

The Frankfurt School's original concern was class. The oppressor was the bourgeoisie. The oppressed was the proletariat. The culture industry served the interests of capital by producing workers who identified with the system that exploited them.

The American adaptation of this framework, developed through the 1970s and 1980s in university humanities and social science departments, substituted different variables. Class remained but was joined by race and gender as primary axes of oppression. The oppressor was no longer just the capitalist class but white men. The oppressed were women, racial minorities, and eventually anyone who could claim membership in a marginalized group. The culture industry now served patriarchy as well as capital, the system of male dominance that, in this framework, structured every dimension of social life.

Before proceeding, the grievances that drove this adaptation deserve honest acknowledgment, because this book cannot be read as dismissing them. In 1960, American women could not obtain a credit card in their own name. They were formally excluded from most professional schools. They were routinely paid less than men for identical work with no legal remedy. Domestic violence was treated as a private family matter by law enforcement. Marital rape was not a crime in most states. Sexual harassment in the workplace had no legal definition or recourse. These were not marginal complaints or ideological constructions. They were documented institutional realities that produced real damage to real women across generations. The movement that identified and challenged these conditions produced genuine improvements in American life that this book does not dispute and does not wish to reverse.

What this book argues is that the academic framework built to address those genuine grievances did not stop at the grievances. It extended into a complete theory of male identity as the mechanism of oppression, applied that theory through institutional capture at a scale the original grievances did not require, and produced outcomes that served foreign strategic interests rather than American women. The grievances were real. The framework that used them as its foundation became something larger than the grievances justified, and the gap between the two is where the damage documented in this book lives.

The concept of patriarchy as an all-encompassing system of oppression required a theory of masculinity as the mechanism that sustained it. This theory was developed in academic gender studies programs throughout the 1980s and 1990s. Masculinity was not a natural expression of male biology or a set of culturally transmitted virtues. It was a social construction designed to maintain male dominance. The traits associated with masculinity (competitiveness, stoicism, physical courage, protectiveness, willingness to use force) were not admirable qualities that served important social functions. They were the psychological mechanisms through which men perpetuated their own privilege and enforced women's subordination.

The academic term that eventually entered popular culture was "toxic masculinity." The phrase itself is worth examining. Not toxic men. Not men behaving badly. Toxic masculinity, the suggestion that masculinity as a category is inherently pathological, that the traits traditionally associated with being male are the source of the problem rather than the expression of something that, properly channeled, serves essential human purposes.

This framework was not developed in a single paper or a single department. It accumulated across decades of academic production, refined by hundreds of scholars working in dozens of institutions, published in peer-reviewed journals, incorporated into textbooks, taught to graduate students who then taught it to undergraduates who then carried it into every institution they entered.

By the time this framework reached HR departments and corporate diversity training programs in the 2000s and 2010s, it had been laundered through enough layers of academic respectability that most of the people implementing it had no idea where it had come from or what the original theoretical project had been. They knew that toxic masculinity was bad and that addressing it was good and that their professional and social standing depended on treating both of those propositions as settled.

The Education Schools

The most consequential vector for the Frankfurt School's influence on American culture was not the humanities departments where critical theory was developed. It was the schools of education where the people who trained the next generation of teachers were trained.

Teachers College at Columbia University, which sits adjacent to where the Frankfurt School originally landed in New York, became one of the primary sites for the development of what eventually became called critical pedagogy, the application of critical theory to classroom teaching. The foundational figure was Paulo Freire, a Brazilian educator whose 1968 book Pedagogy of the Oppressed became one of the most assigned texts in American education schools and remains so today.

Freire's argument was that traditional education was a form of oppression. He called it the "banking model", teachers depositing knowledge into passive students as if they were empty accounts. True education required helping students recognize their own oppression and develop the "critical consciousness" to challenge the systems that oppressed them. The teacher's role was not to transmit knowledge but to help the student's awakening to their own political situation.

The influence of this framework on American K-12 education is difficult to overstate. Education school curricula across the country incorporated critical pedagogy into the training of every teacher who graduated from those programs. Teachers were trained to see their role not as transmitting the accumulated knowledge and values of their civilization but as helping students critique and resist that civilization. The curriculum was not a body of knowledge to be mastered but a site of political contestation.

The specific consequences for boys and men followed directly from the broader framework. If traditional masculinity was a mechanism of oppression, then the behaviors through which boys expressed developing masculinity (competitiveness, physical play, risk-taking, the formation of hierarchies through contest) were not natural developmental stages to be guided and channeled. They were manifestations of the oppressive system to be identified, named, and corrected.

Boys who acted like boys in classrooms run by teachers trained in this framework were not boys being boys. They were future oppressors exhibiting the early signs of toxic masculinity. The appropriate response was not to provide structured outlets for male energy but to suppress its expression and replace it with the behaviors the framework defined as healthier, which happened to be the behaviors that came more naturally to girls.

The school system that produced this outcome did not do so because teachers hated boys. Most of them did not. It produced this outcome because the framework through which teachers were trained to understand child development defined normal male behavior as a problem. You cannot correct a problem you cannot see as a problem, and you cannot see clearly when the lens through which you look has been ground to a specific shape by seventy years of academic development.

The Seventy-Year Ratchet

From 1923 to the present, the Frankfurt School pipeline is not a conspiracy. It does not require secret meetings or coordinated instructions or any of the apparatus that the word conspiracy implies. Something more mundane and more durable than a conspiracy did this: an intellectual tradition that found a home in American universities, produced generations of students who carried its assumptions into the institutions they entered, and gradually transformed those institutions from inside.

A ratchet is the accurate metaphor. Each generation moved the baseline further in the same direction. Each generation trained the next from within institutions that had already been moved. The movement was never reversed because reversing it would have required the previous generation to acknowledge that the framework it had built its career on was producing outcomes it had not intended or would not endorse. That acknowledgment rarely happens in academic cultures.

Measured in 2026, the result is a university system in which the ratio of liberal to conservative faculty in humanities and social science departments runs between ten to one and twenty to one at most major institutions. A K-12 system in which the curriculum consistently pathologizes male behavior and consistently underserves male learning styles. A media culture in which the assumptions of critical theory are so embedded that most journalists do not recognize them as assumptions at all. A corporate culture in which diversity training programs built on academic frameworks derived from the Frankfurt School are mandatory at most large employers.

None of this required Soviet coordination. The Soviets did not build the Frankfurt School. They did not fund Teachers College. They did not place their agents in humanities departments. They did not need to. The operation was already running. They amplified what was already moving in the right direction, provided resources to the most useful elements, and waited.

The men who made the decision in Moscow in the early 1950s understood that cultural subversion, if done correctly, becomes self-sustaining. You plant the seed. The institution grows it. The graduate students carry it into the next institution. The culture shifts. The shifted culture becomes the new baseline from which the next shift begins.

Seventy years later, the ratchet has turned far enough that the baseline has moved beyond anything the original Frankfurt School theorists would have recognized as their own project. They were serious Marxist intellectuals who believed they were developing a theory of human liberation. What their intellectual descendants built in American institutions is something they would not all have endorsed.

The pipeline argument will be challenged on the grounds that tracing intellectual influence does not establish causation. Ideas spread in all directions. Correlation between Frankfurt School theory and current institutional practice might reflect independent parallel development rather than linear transmission. That objection is worth taking seriously, and this book takes it seriously. The argument here is not that Frankfurt School ideas caused institutional change through a simple pipeline of direct transmission. It is an argument about institutional history: specific ideas were adopted, funded, and systematically incorporated into the training of teachers, journalists, lawyers, and HR professionals over multiple generations, and the institutions those professionals ran then reflected the ideas they had absorbed. That is not a conspiracy claim. It is a description of how institutions change, through the cumulative effect of who gets hired, what they teach, and what assumptions they bring to every decision they make.

What it produced is measurable. The mechanism that delivered it was built to be difficult to counter. That is the subject of the next chapter.

The pipeline ran for seventy years before most people noticed it existed.

Knowing how it worked is the first step toward responding to what it produced.

Chapter 3: The Cult

I did not expect to find what I found when I applied this checklist. I expected partial matches. I found something closer to a complete description.

There is a checklist for identifying destructive groups. A politician did not write it. A commentator with an axe to grind did not write it. Academic researchers who study coercive organizations for a living wrote it, refined it over decades of work with former cult members, and published it through the International Cultic Studies Association. The researchers who built it, Janja Lalich and Michael Langone, are recognized authorities in their field. The checklist is used by mental health professionals, exit counselors, and cult researchers worldwide.

It has twelve criteria.

What follows is the application of those twelve criteria, one by one, to the belief system that the previous two chapters documented: the ideology that arrived through the Frankfurt School pipeline, was delivered through American educational institutions, and is now enforced through corporate HR departments, campus speech codes, and social media pile-ons.

The objection that the criteria were designed for formal coercive groups rather than diffuse ideological movements deserves a direct answer before the chapter proceeds. Lalich and Langone themselves have addressed this. Their framework has been applied to political movements, therapeutic systems, and institutional cultures in peer-reviewed literature with their explicit endorsement. The criteria describe a structure of psychological control. The question the chapter asks is whether that structure is present. Whether it appears in a compound or a corporation or a university system does not change what the structure is or what it does to the people inside it. One further clarification: applying these criteria is a diagnostic act, not an accusatory one. The chapter does not argue that anyone deliberately built a cult or intended to produce coercive control. It argues that a structure with the documented properties of coercive control exists, that it produces the documented outcomes coercive control produces, and that naming the structure accurately is the first step toward understanding why those outcomes are so difficult to counter through ordinary argument.

Read each criterion. Then read the application. Then decide for yourself whether the match is coincidental.

Criterion 1: *Excessively zealous and unquestioning commitment to the doctrine*

The Lalich-Langone description: the group displays excessively zealous and unquestioning commitment to its leader, and regards its belief system, ideology, and practices as the Truth, as law.

The application: In 2008, Barack Obama and Hillary Clinton both stated publicly that marriage was between a man and a woman. In 2012, Obama announced his position had "evolved." By 2015, expressing the position that both of them had held publicly seven years earlier was sufficient grounds for termination at most major American corporations. By 2020, it was sufficient grounds for social destruction on social media and professional cancellation in most cultural institutions.

That is not a cultural shift. A cultural shift takes generations. What happened between 2008 and 2020 is the adoption speed of a doctrine, not the evolution speed of a society. Positions that went from mainstream to unsayable in twelve years did not get there through persuasion. They got there through the enforcement mechanisms of a belief system that treats its own conclusions as settled law and treats disagreement as moral failure.

The unquestioning commitment extends beyond any specific position to the framework itself. Question a specific policy and you can sometimes survive. Question the framework that produced the policy and you cannot. The framework is not subject to debate. It is the lens through which all debate must be conducted. That is not how honest intellectual discourse works. It is how dogma works.

Criterion 2: *Questioning, doubt, and dissent are discouraged or punished*

The Lalich-Langone description: questioning, doubt, and dissent are discouraged or even punished.

The application: In 2017, James Damore was fired from Google for writing a memo that questioned whether the gender gap in tech employment was entirely the result of discrimination. The memo cited peer-reviewed research. It was careful in its language. It explicitly stated it was not arguing that women were inferior. None of that mattered. The act of questioning the framework was treated as equivalent to endorsing the conclusion the framework most feared, and the punishment was immediate and public.

Damore is not an isolated case. He is an example of a pattern that plays out at every level of American institutional life, from the corporate employee fired for a social media post to the university professor who loses tenure consideration for publishing research whose conclusions the ideology dislikes, to the high school teacher disciplined for assigning a book that contains a perspective the framework defines as harmful.

Asymmetry is the tell. You can question the ideology's opponents without consequence. You cannot question the ideology without consequence. In any honest intellectual environment, the opposite would be true. Questioning what you already believe is the foundation of rational inquiry. Punishing the questioning of a belief system is the foundation of a cult.

Criterion 3: *Mind-altering practices used to suppress doubt*

Criterion five: mind-altering practices such as meditation, chanting, speaking in tongues, denunciation sessions, or debilitating work routines are used in excess and serve to suppress doubts about the group and its leader.

Updating these criteria for a secular context requires translation. The specific practices secular institutional context. The function is identical. Land acknowledgments at the opening of every public meeting. Mandatory diversity training that requires participants to confess their privilege and commit to the framework's remedies. Preferred pronoun declarations that function as daily ideological affirmation regardless of whether the speaker believes in the underlying theory. Struggle sessions on college campuses where students are required to examine and confess their complicity in systems of oppression.

The phrase "struggle session" is not an accident. It comes directly from Maoist China, where it described a specific practice of public self-criticism and denunciation used to enforce ideological conformity. The practice was imported wholesale, stripped of its explicitly Maoist branding, and repackaged as consciousness-raising, sensitivity training, and implicit bias workshops. The function is the same. You repeat the ritual. The repetition suppresses doubt. The suppression of doubt reinforces commitment. The reinforced commitment makes the next round of ritual easier to accept.

Ask anyone who has sat through a mandatory diversity training whether they felt free to express skepticism about the framework being presented. Ask whether the room felt like a space for honest intellectual inquiry or a space where the correct conclusions had already been determined and the session existed to produce public commitment to them.

You already know the answer.

Criterion 4: Leadership dictates how members must think, act, and feel

Criterion six: leadership dictates, sometimes in great detail, how members should think, act, and feel.

At American universities, speech codes now specify which words and which ideas cannot be expressed. Corporate diversity policies go further: not just behaviors but beliefs must be publicly affirmed as a condition of employment. HR departments conduct investigations not just into actions but into expressed opinions, social media posts, and private conversations reported by colleagues.

Pronoun management is the clearest example. You are not merely asked to avoid slurs. You are required to use specific words in specific contexts, and the failure to use them correctly is treated not as a breach of etiquette but as an act of violence. The word "violence" is doing important work there. Violence justifies a response that mere rudeness does not. By defining incorrect pronoun use as violence, the framework justifies the institutional response that follows.

Dictation extends to feelings. Microaggression theory holds that the intent of the speaker is irrelevant. What matters is how the listener feels. If a member of a protected group reports feeling harmed by a statement, the statement is harmful regardless of what the speaker intended or what the statement said. This is not a standard of conduct. It is a standard that makes the feelings of specific group members the arbiter of acceptable speech for everyone else. Leadership dictating how members must feel, extended to the entire population of an institution.

Criterion 5: The group is elitist, claiming special status

Criterion seven: the group is elitist, claiming a special, exalted status for itself, its leader, and members. The group and its leader have a special mission to save humanity.

Applied here: the woke framework divides humanity into the enlightened and the unenlightened. Those who have "done the work" of examining their privilege and committing to the framework's remedies occupy a moral position unavailable to those who have not. The language of being "woke" is itself a description of a special state of consciousness that the majority of people have not achieved.

The moral hierarchy is explicit and ranked. At the top are those who have not only adopted the framework but actively work to spread it. Below them are those who have adopted it but remain passive. Below them are the uninitiated who might yet be saved. At the bottom are the actively resistant, who are not merely wrong but evil, not merely misguided but complicit in oppression.

The secular Calvinist structure is exact. There are the elect and the damned. Membership in the elect is demonstrated through the public performance of ideological commitment. The performance is never complete because there is always more privilege to examine, more complicity to confess, more work to be done. The goal recedes as you approach it, which keeps the member in a permanent state of striving that prevents them from ever feeling secure enough to question the framework that defines the goal.

That is not social justice. That is a status game with a moral vocabulary, and it serves the same function in the ideology that the concept of spiritual election served in the most authoritarian strains of Calvinist theology. You are saved. They are not. The distinction is permanent and visible to those who know how to look.

Criterion 6: *Polarized us-versus-them mentality*

Criterion ten: the group has a polarized us-versus-them mentality, which may cause conflict with the wider society.

Every social question gets divided along a single axis. Oppressor and oppressed. Privileged and marginalized. Those who are part of the problem and those who are part of the solution. The axis does not permit middle positions. You are either actively anti-racist or you are racist. You are either with the framework or you are against it, and being against it is not a matter of intellectual disagreement. It is a moral failing that places you in the category of oppressor.

Underneath this, the Marxist structure is visible. The Frankfurt School replaced the bourgeoisie and the proletariat with oppressor groups and oppressed groups, but the binary logic is identical. History is a struggle between two sides. There is no neutral position. Failing to actively support the oppressed is functionally equivalent to supporting the oppressor. The fence does not exist.

The consequences for social cohesion are exactly what you would predict. A society organized around a framework that divides every human interaction into oppressor and oppressed cannot maintain the civic trust that democratic governance requires. You cannot have productive disagreement with someone the framework has defined as your oppressor. You cannot extend good faith to someone who, by definition of the framework, is acting in bad faith toward you. The us-versus-them mentality does not just cause conflict with the wider society, as the Lalich-Langone criterion notes. It makes resolution of that conflict structurally impossible within the framework's own terms.

Which, from the perspective of foreign actors who benefit from American social division, is exactly the point.

Criterion 7: *The leader or group has a special mission to save humanity*

Criterion eleven: the group has a special mission to save humanity.

Social justice as secular eschatology. The arc of history bending toward justice. The believers as the vanguard of inevitable moral progress. This language is not metaphorical. It is the explicit framing of the movement's own self-description.

Being "on the right side of history" performs the same function as being in a state of grace. It provides absolute moral confidence to the believer and absolute moral condemnation to the opponent, without requiring any specific argument to be made or evidence to be evaluated. History has already rendered judgment. Those who resist the framework are not just wrong. They are fighting against the direction of history itself, which is as close to the concept of fighting against God as a secular ideology can get.

Missionary impulse follows directly. If you possess the truth and others do not, and if the stakes are the liberation of humanity from oppression, then spreading the truth is not optional. It is an obligation. The aggressive expansion of diversity training into every institutional space, the insistence that every curriculum include the framework's perspective, the demand that every public figure and institution declare explicit commitment to the ideology's positions, these are not expressions of social concern. They are the evangelical imperative of a belief system that has defined itself as the vehicle of human salvation.

Salvation, in this framework, means liberation from oppression. The framework defines what oppression is. The framework defines what liberation looks like. The framework defines who is saved and who is not. And the framework defines itself as the only mechanism through which salvation is available. That is the complete structure of a religious soteriology, rebuilt in secular vocabulary and deployed in the institutional spaces that critical theory spent seventy years capturing.

Criterion 8: *Members are manipulated into pursuing group goals*

The Lalich-Langone description: the group uses deceptive practices to recruit members or expand its influence.

The application: the recruitment mechanism for this ideology is not a meeting or a pamphlet. It is education. Students enter universities to learn skills and develop knowledge that will allow them to build careers. They encounter the framework as the organizing assumption of their courses, their residential life programming, their student orientation, their administrative communications. It is not presented as one perspective among many. It is presented as the framework through which all perspectives must be evaluated.

A student who arrives at a university without the ideological framework and leaves four years later with it has not been persuaded through honest intellectual competition. They have been immersed in an environment that treated the framework as the water and every other perspective as something that needed to be explained and justified against that baseline. The immersion is the manipulation. It works not through deception in the traditional sense but through the systematic management of the intellectual environment in which the student develops.

The same mechanism operates in corporate onboarding, where new employees encounter the framework as institutional policy before they have developed relationships or standing that would allow them to question it. It operates in K-12 education, where children encounter it before they have the cognitive development to evaluate it critically. It operates in the mandatory training that turns disagreement into a career risk and agreement into a professional obligation.

You do not recruit people to a cult by telling them it is a cult. You recruit them by presenting the cult's assumptions as the natural, obvious, and morally necessary starting point for all serious thinking.

Criterion 9: *Members are expected to devote inordinate amounts of time to the group*

Criterion twelve: members are expected to devote inordinate amounts of time to the group and its activities.

Identity colonization is the application. The ideology does not ask for some of your time. It asks for all of your self-concept. Every social interaction becomes an opportunity to perform ideological commitment. Every personal relationship is evaluated through the lens of the framework. Every entertainment choice, dietary decision, purchasing behavior, and social media post becomes a site of political expression that must be consistent with the framework's demands.

The exhaustion this produces is documented and real. Researchers studying ideologically motivated social media use have found that heavy users of social justice-oriented content report higher rates of anxiety, depression, and burnout than comparable populations. The framework demands constant vigilance because the category of oppressive behavior keeps expanding, the bar for acceptable performance of commitment keeps rising, and the social consequences of falling short keep intensifying.

Rest from the ideology is not available because the ideology has defined the personal as political. There is no private space where the framework does not apply. There is no conversation that is not, at some level, a political act. There is no relationship that is not structured by the power dynamics the framework describes. The total claim on the member's time, attention, and identity is not a side effect of the ideology. It is a feature. A member who has no self that exists outside the group's framework has no self from which to evaluate the group.

Criterion 10: *Members are encouraged to report on each other*

Criterion nine: members are encouraged to report one another's undesirable behavior to the leadership.

Bias reporting systems at universities now allow students to anonymously report peers and faculty for statements they find offensive. Corporate ethics hotlines encourage employees to report colleagues for expressions of opinion that conflict with company diversity policies. Social media functions as a distributed surveillance network in which anyone's public statements can be captured, decontextualized, and submitted to the pile-on machinery that destroys professional reputations.

Call-out culture is the most sophisticated version. that operates within ideologically committed communities. A member who fails to perform commitment at the required level, who uses the wrong term, who fails to amplify the right message, who is perceived to have given insufficient support to a marginalized person in a conflict, is subject to public denunciation by other members. The denunciation is not private. It is performed publicly, in front of the community, because the public performance of the denunciation is itself a demonstration of the denouncer's commitment.

At its peak, the East German Stasi had one informant for every sixty-three citizens. Social media, in communities organized around this ideology, produces something approaching one potential informant per member, available twenty-four hours a day, with a global reach and no due process. The surveillance is not incidental to the ideology. The ideology requires it because the ideology's enforcement depends on the constant visibility of everyone's performance of commitment.

Criterion 11: Outsiders are viewed as evil, corrupt, or lost

Criterion ten: the group has a polarized us-versus-them mentality with the outside world viewed as evil, lost, or corrupt.

Labels are the tell. Anyone outside the framework is not merely wrong. They are labeled. Racist. Sexist. Transphobe. Bigot. Nazi. The labels are not descriptive. They are not the conclusion of an argument that examined specific evidence and reached a specific finding. They are the application of a category that, once applied, ends the conversation and justifies any response.

The label works as a cult label works. Once you have been labeled, you cannot defend yourself without the defense being taken as further evidence of the label's accuracy. Deny being a racist and you are demonstrating white fragility, which proves the label. Deny being a transphobe and you are exhibiting the very resistance to accountability that the label describes. The label is self-sealing. The only permitted response is confession, which the ideology treats as the beginning of the long work of becoming a better ally.

The practical consequence is the elimination of good-faith disagreement as a social possibility. You cannot disagree with the framework in good faith because the framework has defined disagreement as evidence of the label's accuracy. You cannot bring evidence against the framework's conclusions because the framework has defined the criteria for acceptable evidence in ways that exclude the most challenging counter-examples. You cannot appeal to principles the framework does not share because the framework has defined its own principles as the only legitimate ones.

This is not intellectual discourse. It is the complete closure of inquiry that characterizes the most authoritarian belief systems humans have ever built.

Criterion 12: *Former members are punished or shunned*

The Lalich-Langone description: the group is elitist with those who leave or are ejected labeled as spiritual failures, evil, or traitors.

The application: apostasy from this ideology is punished with a thoroughness that most traditional religious organizations would envy. The public figure who changes their position on a framework-sanctioned issue does not simply lose an argument. They lose their platform, their professional network, their publishing contracts, their speaking engagements, and often their career. The punishment is not proportional to the degree of apostasy. It is total and it is public.

Brendan Eich was removed as CEO of Mozilla in 2014 for a donation he had made to a California ballot measure six years earlier. He had not acted on the position in any capacity as CEO. He had not imposed it on employees. The donation had been a legal act of private political expression. None of that mattered. The act of having held the position was sufficient. The punishment was immediate and it was complete.

J.K. Rowling wrote a series of books that made millions of children love reading and then expressed a view about biological sex that the framework defines as heresy. The campaign against her has run for years, involves the participation of major publishing houses, entertainment companies, and academic institutions, and shows no signs of reaching a resolution that does not involve her complete capitulation to a position she does not hold. The scale of the response to one author's expressed opinion about a specific question is exactly what the Lalich-Langone criterion predicts for a group that treats former members as traitors.

Leaving costs everything by design, because the cost of leaving must exceed the benefit of leaving. If leaving the ideology cost nothing, people would leave when the demands became too great. By making leaving professionally and socially catastrophic, the ideology ensures that members who have doubts suppress them. The suppression of doubts produces more committed members. More committed members produce more effective enforcement. More effective enforcement raises the cost of leaving further.

The ratchet turns.

What the Match Means

Twelve criteria. Twelve matches.

Lalich and Langone did not design their checklist to describe political ideologies. It was designed to identify destructive groups that exercise coercive psychological control over their members. The researchers who built it were thinking about organizations like the People's Temple and NXIVM and Heaven's Gate, groups that used psychological manipulation to override the independent judgment of their members and produce compliance through manufactured dependency rather than honest persuasion.

The ideology documented in this chapter was not built by a charismatic leader in a compound. It was built over seventy years by serious academic thinkers, refined in graduate seminars, legitimized by prestigious institutions, and delivered through the most trusted educational and professional systems in the country. It does not feel like a cult from the inside because the people inside it have spent their entire educational lives in an environment where its assumptions were treated as the baseline of rational discourse.

That is what makes it more dangerous than a conventional cult, not less. A conventional cult requires you to leave your existing life and join a new community. This ideology requires only that you go to college, get a job at a major corporation, and consume mainstream media. The delivery mechanism is indistinguishable from ordinary life in twenty-first century America.

Russia did not build this ideology. The Frankfurt School was not a KGB operation. The long march through institutions was not directed from Moscow. But the men who decided in the early 1950s to fight American culture instead of American military power knew exactly what they were looking for: a self-replicating system for degrading American confidence in its own values, delivered through America's own institutions, by America's own people, in terms that Americans would accept as their own intellectual development.

They found it. They amplified it. They waited.

The twelve criteria are not a metaphor. They are a diagnostic.

Part Two: The Payload

What the weapon does to men and boys.

Chapter 4: The Chemical Attack

In 1960, the Food and Drug Administration approved the first oral contraceptive for use in the United States. By 1965, six and a half million American women were taking it. By 1970, that number had doubled. By the end of the decade, the birth control pill was the most prescribed drug in the country.

Nobody running the cultural subversion operation in Moscow planned this. Nobody in the Frankfurt School wrote a paper about synthetic hormones. The pill arrived through its own history, driven by its own advocates, funded by its own philanthropists, approved by its own regulatory process. It had nothing to do with Soviet active measures.

It did not need to. The operation that was trying to alter the hormonal and behavioral baseline of American women did not need to plant the pill. The pill planted itself. What the operation needed was already happening, driven by entirely different forces, producing effects that compounded with everything the cultural operation was doing at the same time.

This chapter is about those effects. Not about intent. Not about conspiracy. About what the science says happened when you alter the hormonal environment of half the population for sixty years and what it means for the relationship between men and women that the operation was at the same time trying to destroy.

Before the science: a word about what to do with it. The environmental causes documented in this chapter (endocrine disruptors in plastics, synthetic hormones in the water supply, agricultural runoff) are not problems any individual can solve through personal behavior. They require policy responses at a scale beyond what any man reading this chapter can produce on his own. The behavioral factors that affect hormonal health (resistance training, body weight, sleep, alcohol) are within individual control and are addressed in Chapter 12. This chapter is about understanding the landscape, not about producing individual anxiety or assigning individual blame. A man who reads this chapter and concludes that his hormonal health is determined by forces entirely outside his control will have misread it. So will a man who concludes that personal discipline can fully counter what the environment is doing. The truth is between those positions, and Chapter 12 is where the practical part lives.

What the Pill Does

The birth control pill works by delivering synthetic versions of estrogen and progesterone that suppress ovulation. Most women who take it know this. What fewer know is what else those synthetic hormones do, because that information was not prominent in the marketing, not emphasized in the prescribing conversations, and not the subject of the kind of sustained public health attention you would expect given the scale of the intervention.

Start with the progestins. The synthetic progesterone compounds in many oral contraceptives are not chemically identical to natural progesterone. Many of them are derived from testosterone. They are androgenic compounds, meaning they have testosterone-like properties. The androgenic properties of different pill formulations vary considerably. This is documented in the pharmacological literature. It simply never made it into the public conversation about what the pill does to the women taking it.

The most robustly documented behavioral effect is on mood. A 2016 study published in JAMA Psychiatry covering over one million Danish women across thirteen years found that women using hormonal contraceptives had a significantly higher rate of subsequent depression diagnosis and antidepressant use than women not using them. The study was large, longitudinal, and methodologically rigorous. It is not a fringe finding. It has not changed the standard prescribing conversation.

A separate body of research has examined whether hormonal contraceptives alter women's preferences for masculine partners. This research is worth describing carefully because it has been widely cited, frequently misrepresented, and is now the subject of genuine scientific dispute. The earlier studies, conducted in the 1990s and 2000s, suggested that women on the pill preferred less masculine facial features than women not on the pill, and that this difference tracked the suppression of the mid-cycle hormonal shift that normally increases preferences for masculine traits during the fertile phase. These findings were replicated across multiple laboratories and received substantial attention.

The honest account of where this research now stands is more complicated. A 2019 study published in PLOS One found no evidence that pill users had weaker preferences for male facial masculinity. More consequentially, a 2025 double-blind randomized controlled trial, 340 women, pre-registered analysis plan, objective hormonal measurements, the most rigorous design ever applied to this question, found no meaningful difference in facial preferences between women taking oral contraceptives and those on a placebo. The researchers concluded that earlier positive findings were likely driven by small samples and flexible analytical strategies that increase false positive rates. This is the current state of the evidence: the earlier findings have not survived the most rigorous testing.

This chapter does not present the mate preference claim as established science. It presents it as a hypothesis that was suggested by early research, that has not survived the gold-standard test, and that should therefore be treated as unresolved. The population-level extrapolation, that sixty years of widespread pill use measurably shifted aggregate female mate preferences and downstream male behavior, is not supported by the current evidence and this book does not make that claim.

What the pill research does establish, beyond reasonable dispute, is this: a medication taken daily by tens of millions of women for sixty years has documented effects on mood, documented effects on depression risk, documented effects on the hormonal environment of the water supply, and a biological mechanism capable of affecting mate preferences whose behavioral effects at the population level have not been adequately studied. The civilization-scale experiment was conducted. The monitoring infrastructure to understand its full effects was never built. That is the informed consent failure, and it is real regardless of whether the mate preference hypothesis proves correct.

The Testosterone Decline: What the Studies Show

Male testosterone levels in the United States and other Western countries have been declining for decades. This is not a matter of scientific dispute. The foundational study was published by Thomas Travison and colleagues at the New England Research Institutes in the Journal of Clinical Endocrinology and Metabolism in 2007. The study followed randomly selected men in the Boston area across three measurement periods spanning 1987 to 2004. The finding was an age-independent population-level decline of approximately 1.2 percent per year. A man of thirty in 2004 had measurably lower testosterone than a man of thirty in 1987, controlling for age, obesity, smoking, alcohol use, and other lifestyle factors. The accompanying editorial from Boston University's

Shalender Bhasin called the magnitude disquieting and stated that it was not explained by the usual suspects.

The Travison finding has been independently corroborated multiple times. A 2013 study published in PLOS One followed 991 Air Force veterans over twenty years and found a population-level decline independent of body weight and marital status. The researchers stated plainly that they could not identify a reason for the secular decline. A 2025 meta-analysis published in the Journal of Endocrinological Investigation, covering 1.5 million subjects across studies from 1971 to 2024, confirmed that the negative linear trend between testosterone levels and year of measurement persists. The decline is not a single study's finding. It is the consistent result across multiple independent research groups using different populations and different methodologies over nearly forty years of data.

The decline is not explained by aging, because the studies control for age. It is not explained by obesity, though obesity independently reduces testosterone, the trend persists when controlling for body mass. It is not explained by changes in smoking rates or alcohol consumption. What the researchers have found, and what they state plainly in the literature, is that they have not identified the cause.

What the research has found is a collection of probable contributors, the most extensively documented of which are endocrine-disrupting chemicals, synthetic compounds that interfere with the body's hormonal signaling systems. The specific mechanisms are documented at the molecular level in peer-reviewed research.

Bisphenol A, commonly called BPA, is a plasticizer used in polycarbonate plastics, epoxy resins, food packaging, and the linings of canned goods. It is detectable in the urine of over ninety percent of Americans, according to biomonitoring data. BPA binds to estrogen receptors and interferes with the hypothalamic-pituitary-testicular axis, the hormonal cascade that governs testosterone production. Cross-sectional studies have found that higher urinary BPA concentrations are associated with a ten to fifteen percent reduction in blood testosterone levels. A 2024 meta-analysis in Toxics covering eighteen studies found that urinary BPA concentration was negatively correlated with sperm concentration and total sperm count.

Phthalates are a class of plasticizers used in flexible plastics, personal care products, food packaging, and hundreds of consumer goods. They are among the most pervasive chemical exposures in the modern environment, with children showing two to four times higher concentrations than adults. The mechanism of action on testosterone production is documented: phthalates interfere with the Steroidogenic Acute Regulatory protein (the StAR protein) that transports cholesterol into the mitochondria, the necessary first step in testosterone synthesis. Men in the highest quartile of urinary phthalate metabolites show testosterone levels approximately twelve to fifteen percent lower than men in the lowest quartile, documented in multiple studies including a NHANES-based study of 1,262 American men. The association persists after controlling for other variables.

These are not trace effects from exotic exposures. They are measurable hormonal differences associated with the routine daily exposure patterns of ordinary Americans to chemicals present in food packaging, water bottles, canned goods, and personal care products that are ubiquitous in the modern environment. The regulatory standards that govern acceptable exposure levels were set without knowledge of the endocrine disruption mechanisms that subsequent research has documented.

The water supply point deserves to sit on the page for a moment. The synthetic hormones that millions of American women take every day to prevent ovulation do not disappear when excreted. They enter the sewage system. They survive water treatment at measurable concentrations. They flow back into rivers and reservoirs. They end up in tap water. Fish in waterways downstream from major population centers show measurable hormonal disruption. The male fish feminize. The female fish masculinize. The human population downstream drinks the water.

Nobody designed this. Nobody planned it. The pharmaceutical companies that developed oral contraceptives were not thinking about what would happen to the testosterone levels of men sixty years later. The municipalities that built water treatment plants in the 1950s were not designing systems capable of removing synthetic hormones that did not yet exist. The farmers using hormone treatments in livestock operations were not running a coordinated campaign to alter the endocrine environment of the American male population.

They did not need to. The cumulative effect of millions of uncoordinated decisions, made over decades, for entirely different reasons, was a measurable shift in the hormonal environment of American men in exactly the direction that the cultural operation was at the same time trying to produce through entirely different means.

What Lower Testosterone Produces

I want to be honest about how I react to the data in this section. I read it and I got angry. Not at the men whose levels have dropped. At the conditions that produced the drop.

Testosterone is not just a sex hormone. It is a behavioral and psychological hormone with documented effects on confidence, risk tolerance, competitive drive, physical energy, and the willingness to defend oneself and others against external threats. The research literature on testosterone's behavioral effects is extensive and not seriously contested in its broad outlines, even though specific mechanisms and effect sizes remain subjects of ongoing study.

Higher testosterone is associated with greater willingness to take risks, greater competitiveness, greater resistance to social pressure, greater assertiveness in conflict, and greater physical energy. Lower testosterone is associated with the reverse of each of those. Men with chronically low testosterone report lower energy, lower confidence, greater social anxiety, reduced competitive drive, and reduced motivation to pursue goals that require sustained effort against resistance.

Now consider what the Frankfurt School pipeline was producing in American institutions at the same time that testosterone levels were declining. The pipeline was producing an ideology that pathologized male competitiveness, male assertiveness, male risk-taking, male resistance to social pressure, and male willingness to use force in defense of something. The cultural operation was labeling the behaviors associated with higher testosterone as toxic. The chemical changes were reducing the hormonal substrate that produces those behaviors.

The two operations, one deliberate and one entirely accidental, were pulling in the same direction. The ideology told men that masculine traits were dangerous and shameful. The hormonal environment reduced the biological drive to express those traits. The result was a male population that was at the same time being told that the behaviors testosterone produces are wrong and experiencing reduced biological pressure to produce those behaviors in the first place.

You could not have designed a more effective combination if you had tried. The men who ran the cultural operation in Moscow did not try. They did not know about the testosterone decline. The testosterone decline did not know about the cultural operation. They converged on the same target through entirely different mechanisms and produced compounding effects that neither would have produced alone.

The Informed Consent Failure

In 1960, when the FDA approved the first oral contraceptive, the known risks were primarily cardiovascular. Blood clots. Stroke. Heart attack in women who smoked. These risks were documented, disclosed, and weighed against the substantial benefit of effective pregnancy prevention. The decision millions of women made to take the pill was a reasonable decision based on the information available.

The information available did not include the depression research, because that research had not been conducted. The JAMA Psychiatry study that followed over a million Danish women for thirteen years and found a significantly elevated rate of depression diagnosis and antidepressant use among hormonal contraceptive users was published in 2016, fifty-six years after approval. It did not include any serious discussion of what the long-term population-level effects of mass hormonal alteration might be on the hormonal environment of the water supply, on birth rates, or on family formation. Those questions were not asked because the framework in which the pill was developed and approved did not think to ask them.

This is not an argument against contraception. It is an argument that the conversation about what hormonal contraceptives do was systematically incomplete and that the incompleteness has consequences that are now measurable. Women deserve complete information about what they are taking. The depression research is not fringe. It is large, longitudinal, and rigorously conducted. It has not changed the standard prescribing conversation.

This silence is not a conspiracy. It is the product of a medical culture that approved the pill for one purpose, documented its effectiveness at that purpose, and did not build the systematic long-term monitoring infrastructure that would have caught the psychological effects earlier. Combined with a political environment in which questioning any aspect of contraceptive access was treated as an attack on women's rights, the silence was overdetermined. The questions that needed to be asked were questions that nobody in a position to ask them was incentivized to ask.

Two Attacks, Same Target

Two separate chemical channels ran alongside the cultural one. mechanisms that were both unplanned, both uncoordinated with the cultural operation, and both pulling in the same direction.

First: the testosterone decline. Documented, not seriously contested, and its behavioral consequences are real. A male population with measurably lower testosterone has less competitive drive, less physical energy, lower confidence, reduced assertiveness, and reduced motivation to pursue goals that require sustained effort against resistance. The Frankfurt School pipeline was at the same time producing an ideology that pathologized precisely those traits. The cultural operation told men that masculine behaviors were toxic. The chemical environment was reducing the hormonal substrate that produces those behaviors. Two forces, one deliberate and one entirely accidental, converging on the same target.

Second is more speculative. The pill's documented effects on mood and depression risk are real and underappreciated. The biological mechanism by which synthetic hormones could affect mate preferences is real and documented at the pharmacological level. Whether that mechanism produces measurable population-level effects on actual partner selection is the question the research has not yet answered reliably. The book does not claim it has. What the book does claim is that a civilization-scale hormonal intervention was conducted without the monitoring infrastructure required to understand its full effects, and that the effects it has produced (including the documented increase in depression risk) have not received the public health attention they deserve.

The honest framing is this: the testosterone decline is established and its behavioral consequences compound with the cultural operation in ways that are documentable. The pill's effects beyond depression risk remain inadequately studied. Both represent failures of monitoring at a scale that should be unacceptable. Neither required any coordination with the forces that were deliberately targeting American masculinity through other means. They simply ran in the same direction, producing compounding damage that nobody designed and nobody measured.

What This Is Not

This chapter will be misread. Let me be specific about what it is not saying before the misreading happens.

It is not saying that women should not have access to contraception. Contraception is a genuine benefit that has genuinely improved the lives of hundreds of millions of women. The argument here is about complete information, not about restriction.

It is not saying that the women who used hormonal contraceptives did anything wrong. They made reasonable decisions based on the information they were given. The failure of informed consent belongs to the medical and regulatory systems that did not provide complete information, not to the women who reasonably trusted those systems.

Here I have to be honest about what I do not know. The relationship between hormonal contraception and long-term partner selection is contested territory. The early research suggested an effect. The replication record is mixed. I find the hypothesis plausible enough to document and contested enough that I am not certain of it. I am certain the question has not been asked with enough seriousness by the institutions that should be asking it.

It is not saying that the mate preference hypothesis is established science. The earlier studies suggested an effect that has not survived the most rigorous testing. This book does not make the claim that the pill measurably shifted aggregate female mate preferences at the population level. That claim is not supported by the current evidence.

It is not saying that the testosterone decline is the only cause of the changes in male behavior documented in the next chapters. It is one documented factor among several. The cultural operation documented in the preceding chapters is a larger and more direct factor. The economic changes that eliminated the employment base for working-class men is another. The testosterone decline is the biological dimension running alongside the cultural and economic ones, compounding their effects on a population that was already under pressure from multiple directions.

What this chapter is saying is precise. The chemical environment of American men changed significantly over the past sixty years through documented mechanisms (endocrine-disrupting chemicals at concentrations measurably associated with reduced testosterone) in ways that nobody planned, through routes that nobody monitored systematically. The hormonal environment of American women also changed, with documented effects on depression risk and other psychological outcomes that received less attention than they deserved. The combination of these chemical changes with the cultural operation documented in the preceding chapters produced outcomes that serve the same strategic purpose as a deliberate attack, whether or not any deliberate attack was responsible for the chemical dimension.

The operation had a biological dimension as well as a cultural one. That changes what a response requires. You cannot counter a chemical effect through argument. You cannot restore a hormonal environment through ideology. The response has to address what happened, at every level where it happened.

Nobody designed the chemical attack. Nobody needed to. The results were the same.

Chapter 5: The Classroom

In 1979, the year I started paying close attention to how institutions worked, the average American elementary school classroom had a roughly even split of male and female teachers. Not perfectly even, but close enough that a boy moving through the system would encounter adult men in meaningful numbers throughout his education. Men who taught, coached, supervised, and modeled what adult male behavior looked like in a professional context.

By 2024, men represented less than twenty-three percent of the K-12 teaching workforce. In elementary schools, the number was lower. In early childhood education, men had nearly disappeared from the workforce entirely, representing less than three percent of preschool and kindergarten teachers nationally.

That shift did not happen because men lost interest in working with children. It happened because the institutional environment of American education shifted in ways that made it progressively less hospitable to men, and because the ideological framework documented in the preceding chapters was applied most completely and most consistently in the institutions that train teachers and shape curriculum.

The result is an educational system that a boy entering kindergarten today will spend thirteen years inside before he graduates high school, during which he will be taught almost exclusively by women, according to a curriculum that treats his natural developmental behaviors as problems, in an institutional culture that has absorbed the full framework of the ideology this book documents.

The data on what this produces is available. Nobody in authority wants to talk about it.

The Numbers Nobody Wants to Discuss

Start with the basic achievement data. American boys are now behind American girls on virtually every measurable academic outcome. Boys read at lower levels than girls at every grade. Boys are more likely to repeat a grade. Boys are less likely to graduate high school on time. Boys are less likely to enroll in college. Boys are less likely to complete a four-year degree. The college enrollment gap has been widening for thirty years and now runs at roughly sixty percent female to forty percent male, with projections suggesting it will widen further.

This is not an American anomaly. The same pattern appears across every developed country that has implemented the ideological framework documented in this book. Britain, Canada, Australia, the Nordic countries, everywhere the educational establishment adopted the framework, male academic performance declined relative to female performance. The countries that did not adopt the framework do not show the same gap.

The discipline data compounds the academic data. Boys are suspended from school at more than twice the rate of girls. Boys are expelled at more than three times the rate of girls. Boys are referred to special education at roughly twice the rate of girls. Boys are diagnosed with attention deficit disorders and medicated for them at four times the rate of girls. Every one of these disparities has been widening since the 1980s, tracking the penetration of the ideological framework into educational institutions.

The special education referral data is worth sitting with. When a system consistently identifies boys as requiring special intervention at twice the rate of girls, across every racial and socioeconomic group, across every region of the country, over multiple decades, there are two possible explanations. Either boys have a biological predisposition toward the behaviors that get them referred to special education, or the system has defined normal male behavior as requiring special intervention.

The research does not support the first explanation at the scale the data shows. The second explanation fits the data precisely.

Boys were not broken. The framework that evaluates them decided they were.

What Normal Male Behavior Looks Like

The research on male child development is extensive and consistent across decades and across cultures. Boys develop differently from girls on a predictable timeline. Boys show higher rates of physical activity and physical play. Boys show higher rates of competitive behavior, including aggressive competition. Boys show higher rates of risk-taking. Boys show higher rates of what researchers call rough-and-tumble play, the physical contact play that establishes social hierarchies and teaches conflict resolution through physical means. Boys show lower rates of verbal communication about emotional states and higher rates of emotional communication through action.

None of these differences are pathological. Every human culture that has ever existed has recognized them, accommodated them, and built institutional structures around channeling them productively. The warrior training, the apprenticeships, the team sports, the competitive academic structures, the initiation rites, all of these were built by cultures that understood that male developmental energy needed direction, not suppression.

The American educational system of 2026 has largely abandoned the direction model in favor of the suppression model. The behaviors that male developmental psychology identifies as normal expressions of male developmental energy are treated by the current educational system as problems to be corrected rather than energies to be channeled.

A boy who hits another boy during a dispute on the playground is not necessarily a violent child. He may be a child resolving a conflict through the physical means that his developmental stage makes available to him, in exactly the way that boys have resolved conflicts throughout human history. The appropriate institutional response is to teach him other means of conflict resolution while acknowledging that the physical impulse is normal. The actual institutional response in most American schools is suspension, followed by a behavioral intervention plan, followed in many cases by a referral for evaluation and possible medication.

The medication point requires direct examination. Adderall and Ritalin and their pharmaceutical relatives are being prescribed to American boys at rates that have no historical precedent and no equivalent in countries that have not adopted the same educational framework. The drugs suppress the behavioral characteristics associated with higher testosterone and male developmental energy: physical activity, impulsivity, competitive drive, resistance to sustained sedentary attention tasks. They make boys easier to manage in a classroom environment designed for the behavioral profile of girls.

That is not medicine. That is pharmaceutical compliance enforcement dressed up as treatment.

The Curriculum

The academic achievement gap is not only a behavioral management problem. It is also a curriculum problem. American schools have, over the past four decades, systematically shifted away from the content and pedagogical approaches that research identifies as more effective for male learners and toward the content and pedagogical approaches that research identifies as more effective for female learners.

Reading is the clearest example. Boys read less than girls by every measure, and the gap has been widening. The research on why is not mysterious. Boys and girls show different reading preferences on average. Boys prefer nonfiction, adventure, action, humor, and stories where characters face external challenges and overcome them through competence and courage. Girls show stronger preferences for fiction with relational themes, emotional complexity, and character-driven narratives.

The books assigned in American schools have shifted dramatically toward the second category and away from the first. The adventure narratives, the competence stories, the books where boys could see versions of themselves succeeding through the traits they were developing, these have been systematically removed from curricula on the grounds that they contained violence, promoted problematic masculinity, or failed to represent diverse perspectives. The books that replaced them skew heavily toward the relational, the emotional, and the identity-focused.

Boys who do not find the assigned reading engaging are told they need to read more. The books that would engage them are not on the list. The books on the list do not engage them. The resulting reading gap is then attributed to boys being less academically motivated than girls, which produces interventions focused on changing boys rather than changing the curriculum that is failing them.

The same pattern appears in how history is taught, in how science is framed, in how mathematics is presented. The shift away from content that emphasizes competence, mastery, and the building of things toward content that emphasizes relationships, feelings, and systemic critique has been consistent and deliberate. It was not an accident of curricular fashion. It was the direct application of the critical pedagogy framework that Paulo Freire developed and that Teachers College disseminated through American education schools over fifty years.

Zero Tolerance and the Criminalization of Boyhood

In the 1990s, American schools began implementing zero tolerance disciplinary policies in response to a series of high-profile school shootings. The policies were designed to remove discretion from disciplinary decisions, ensuring that specific behaviors resulted in automatic consequences regardless of context.

The application of zero tolerance policies in practice produced an outcome that the research literature now documents extensively: the systematic criminalization of normal male behavior, especially in the elementary years.

The cases are not obscure. A seven-year-old in Maryland was suspended for chewing a Pop-Tart into a shape that vaguely resembled a gun and pointing it at a classmate. A six-year-old in Colorado was suspended for bringing a plastic toy soldier to school as part of a hat he decorated for an assigned school project. The soldier was holding a gun. A six-year-old in Delaware was suspended and faced expulsion for bringing a camping utensil that included a small knife to school to eat his lunch. A thirteen-year-old in New Mexico was suspended for drawing a picture of a weapon during a free drawing exercise.

These cases are individually absurd. Collectively they describe a system that has decided that any symbolic association with weapons, conflict, or competitive aggression requires institutional intervention regardless of context, intent, or actual harm. The things boys naturally draw, play, and talk about (soldiers, weapons, battles, competition, conflict and its resolution) have been categorized as warning signs requiring response.

The effect on boys is measurable and documented. Boys learn quickly that the things they find interesting, the things they naturally think about and play out, are not acceptable in the institutional context of school. The message they receive is not just that certain behaviors are prohibited. The message is that who they are is prohibited. The interests they arrive with are problems. The games they want to play are threats. The stories they want to tell are dangerous.

A boy who spends six hours a day in an institution that treats his natural interests as threatening does not become less interested in those things. He becomes less willing to show who he is in that institution. He disengages. He stops participating. He does the minimum required to avoid conflict and spends his energy elsewhere. The data on male academic disengagement tracks this pattern exactly.

The Title IX Transformation

Title IX of the Education Amendments of 1972 prohibited sex discrimination in federally funded educational programs. The law's original and most visible application was to athletic programs, requiring schools to provide equivalent athletic opportunities to female students. That application produced real and documented benefits for female athletes.

Over the following five decades, the administrative expansion of Title IX went considerably beyond athletic programs. The Obama administration's 2011 Dear Colleague Letter directed schools receiving federal funding to adjudicate sexual misconduct allegations through a preponderance of evidence standard, a standard significantly lower than the beyond-reasonable-doubt standard used in criminal proceedings, and required schools to complete investigations within sixty days regardless of complexity.

Practical consequences for accused male students were extensively documented over the following decade. Students found responsible under the preponderance standard, which means found more likely than not to have committed the alleged misconduct, faced suspension or expulsion with permanent notations in their academic records, without the procedural protections that the criminal justice system provides to people facing comparably serious consequences. Federal courts found constitutional violations in the processes used by dozens of universities. The accused students who won those cases were overwhelmingly male. The universities that lost them had implemented the processes the Department of Education directed them to implement.

Campus disciplinary machinery that developed around expanded Title IX enforcement was not designed to be neutral. It was designed to respond to what the ideological framework had defined as the primary campus safety problem: male sexual aggression against female students. The framework's assumptions about male behavior were built into the process design. The accused was presumed to pose a threat. The accuser was presumed to be credible. The procedural design reflected those assumptions.

Effects on male students' relationship with their educational institutions was predictable. Young men on campuses where these processes operated learned that their institutional standing was vulnerable to accusation in ways that had no equivalent for female students. The lesson was not just about sexual misconduct proceedings. It was about what the institution thought of them and what they could expect from it.

The Male Teacher Collapse and What It Means

Return to the number that opened this chapter. Less than twenty-three percent of K-12 teachers are male. In elementary education, less than one in five. In early childhood education, almost none.

The research on what male teachers provide to male students is consistent across decades and across countries. Boys with male teachers show higher academic engagement. Boys with male teachers are less likely to be referred for disciplinary action. Boys with male teachers are more likely to express interest in academic subjects stereotypically associated with male competence. Boys with male teachers are more likely to report feeling understood by their teacher.

Male teachers also provide something that research cannot fully quantify but that every person who grew up with a good male teacher can describe: a model. A demonstration that adult men take learning seriously, that intellectual work is compatible with masculinity, that the institution of school is a place where men belong and where male ways of engaging with knowledge are legitimate.

The absence of male teachers does not just deprive boys of that model. It sends a signal about what school is and who it is for. A boy who spends his first eight years of formal education without encountering a single male teacher has been told, without anyone saying it directly, that education is a female domain. That the institution he is required to inhabit for thirteen years is designed by women, for women, and judged by women's standards. That his natural relationship to that institution is as an outsider who must adapt to a culture that was not built for him.

The male teacher collapse is not accidental. Teaching became less attractive to men as the institutional culture of education shifted. Men who entered teaching found themselves in institutions where their professional judgment about male students was systematically discounted, where their disciplinary approaches were more likely to be questioned, where the curriculum they were expected to deliver treated male developmental interests as problems, and where the administrative culture had absorbed the framework that treats male behavior as inherently suspect.

Men who might have become excellent teachers looked at that environment and chose other fields. The ones who stayed were self-selected for comfort with an institutional culture that most men found alienating. The result is a teaching workforce that is predominantly female in a way that reflects a specific ideological orientation, because the men who were most likely to push back against that orientation were the men most likely to leave.

What This Produces at Scale

Run the numbers forward.

Take everything this chapter has documented and run it forward through a generation. Boys entering kindergarten in

2000 are now in their early thirties. They spent thirteen years in an educational system that treated their natural behaviors as problems, assigned them reading they did not connect with, medicated them for being themselves at a rate four times higher than their sisters, exposed them to a disciplinary system that criminalized their play, and taught them almost exclusively by women in an institutional culture that had absorbed the full ideology of the Frankfurt School pipeline.

Those boys became men, and those men are visible in the data. They are the men checking out of higher education. They are the men dropping out of the workforce at rates that have no historical precedent. They are the men living in their parents' basements at thirty, not because they are lazy but because the skills, the confidence, and the institutional relationship that would have prepared them for adult life were systematically undermined by the institutions that were supposed to build them.

The workforce dropout data is damning. Prime-age male labor force participation, men between twenty-five and fifty-four, has been declining for sixty years. The decline accelerated in the 2000s. By 2024, roughly seven million prime-age American men were neither working nor looking for work. This is not cyclical unemployment. These are men who have left the labor market permanently. They are not counted in unemployment statistics. They are not receiving meaningful institutional attention. They are the statistical residue of a generation that the educational system processed and did not prepare.

Suicide data is the hardest number in this chapter. American men die by suicide at four times the rate of American women. The rate has been rising for decades. It is the leading cause of death for men under forty-five. The research on risk factors for male suicide consistently identifies social isolation, lack of purpose, and the absence of institutional belonging as primary contributors. An educational system that spent thirteen years communicating to boys that their natural ways of being were problems produced men who carry that message into adulthood.

Nobody planned this. The teachers who implemented zero tolerance policies were not trying to damage boys. The administrators who adopted the diversity training frameworks were not trying to produce a generation of men without purpose. The curriculum designers who removed adventure narratives were not trying to eliminate male engagement with reading. Each individual decision was made by people who believed they were improving the system.

The aggregate effect of those decisions, accumulated over four decades, is a generation of men who were processed by the educational system and came out the other side missing things that education is supposed to provide: competence, confidence, institutional belonging, the sense that the society they are growing into has a place for them and values what they can contribute.

The Counter-Examples

The damage is documented. So is the alternative.

Schools that have deliberately maintained male-friendly environments, that hire male teachers as a priority, that keep competitive structures in academics and athletics, that channel male energy rather than suppress it, that assign reading that boys want to read, consistently produce better outcomes for male students without producing worse outcomes for female students.

The research on single-sex education for boys is consistent: boys in all-male educational environments show higher academic engagement, higher graduation rates, and lower rates of disciplinary intervention than comparable boys in coeducational environments. The explanation is not that boys learn better without girls present. The explanation is that institutions designed for male learners apply different assumptions about what male behavior means and what male development requires.

Military academies and JROTC programs, which maintain explicitly masculine institutional cultures and clear pathways to male competence and belonging, consistently produce young men with higher rates of academic completion, lower rates of behavioral problems, and stronger civic engagement than comparable young men in conventional educational settings. The institution that communicates to boys that what they are is an asset rather than a problem produces boys who engage with the institution rather than withdrawing from it.

The trades pipeline is the most visible counter-example in the current data. Boys who enter vocational and technical education programs, who learn skills with clear real-world application and clear standards of mastery, who work in environments where competence is measured by whether the thing you built works, show dramatically lower rates of the disengagement and dropout that characterize their peers in conventional academic tracks. The institution that respects male ways of knowing and doing produces men who respect the institution back.

None of this is complicated. None of it requires new research or new theory. It requires only the willingness to look at what the educational system has done to boys over the past forty years, acknowledge that the results are not acceptable, and build something different.

The boys who were failed by the classroom are now the men in the data.

Chapter 6: The New Language

I watched the language shift in real time, over about a decade, in the professional world around me. Not a sudden change. A gradual replacement, word by word, phrase by phrase, until the vocabulary people used to describe ordinary situations had become something I barely recognized.

Words are not neutral. Every culture that has ever tried to control behavior has understood this. You do not just change what people do. You change what people can say, and therefore what they can think, and therefore what they can see.

The ideological framework this book documents is, among other things, a linguistic project. It constructed a vocabulary for talking about men and masculinity that embedded its conclusions in the language itself. Once you adopt the vocabulary, you have already accepted the framework. The argument is over before it begins because the terms of the argument have been defined by one side.

This chapter documents that vocabulary. Where the key terms came from. What assumptions they carry. How they function as a delivery mechanism for the ideology rather than as neutral descriptions of observable reality. And what happens to the men described by this language when the culture around them internalizes it.

This language did not drop from the sky. It was built, deliberately, by people who understood exactly what they were building.

Toxic Masculinity: The Manufacturing of a Phrase

The phrase "toxic masculinity" did not originate in academic gender studies, though that is where it acquired its institutional authority. It originated in the mythopoetic men's movement of the late 1980s and early 1990s, a therapeutic movement associated with writers like Robert Bly that was trying to help men reconnect with a deeper, healthier version of masculinity. In that original context, toxic masculinity referred to the wounded, destructive masculinity that results when men are cut off from positive male initiation and healthy masculine development. It was a term about what happens to men when masculinity goes wrong, not a term about masculinity itself.

The academic gender studies apparatus took the phrase, stripped the original meaning, and rebuilt it as a description of masculinity as such. In the academic usage that spread through university curricula from the 1990s onward, toxic masculinity does not refer to a pathological form of masculinity. It refers to the normative expression of masculinity in Western culture. The toxicity is not an aberration from masculinity. It is masculinity.

That is not a subtle distinction. It is the difference between "some men behave in destructive ways when their development goes wrong" and "masculinity is inherently destructive." The first is a clinical observation. The second is an ideological claim dressed up as a clinical observation.

The American Psychological Association codified the academic usage in its 2018 Guidelines for Psychological Practice with Boys and Men. The guidelines identified traditional masculinity (described as stoicism, competitiveness, dominance, and aggression) as harmful on its face, associated it with negative health outcomes, and directed psychologists to help male patients understand the ways traditional masculine norms were damaging them and others.

Read that slowly. The professional organization that certifies American psychologists issued official guidelines defining the traits historically associated with being a functional adult male as pathological. Not as potentially problematic in excess. As harmful on their face. The guidelines were not fringe. They were the official policy of the APA and were widely covered as a significant professional development.

The therapist who follows those guidelines and the patient who walks into that therapist's office are now operating inside a framework that has defined his masculinity as the problem before he has said a single word about why he came. That is not therapy. That is ideology with a billing code.

Privilege: The Framework That Ends Arguments

The concept of privilege as deployed in the contemporary ideological framework is not the ordinary English word meaning an advantage or benefit. It is a technical term with specific theoretical content that was developed in academic sociology and then exported into popular discourse, where it functions very differently than its academic proponents intended.

In the academic usage, privilege refers to unearned advantages that accrue to members of dominant social groups as a result of systemic structures rather than individual effort. The original formulation by Peggy McIntosh in her 1989 essay White Privilege: Unpacking the Invisible Knapsack was a personal reflection on advantages she had not thought to notice. It was not presented as a complete social theory. It was a prompt for self-examination.

What the popular deployment of the concept does is transform it from a prompt for self-examination into a mechanism for dismissing arguments. The privilege framework in popular use does not say "consider whether your perspective might be shaped by advantages you did not earn." It says "your perspective is invalid because of your identity category."

Applied to men, privilege functions as follows. A man who disagrees with any claim made by the ideological framework about men can be told he is speaking from male privilege, which means his disagreement reflects his inability to see his own unearned advantages rather than the quality of his argument. The claim is unfalsifiable. There is no argument a man can make that cannot be attributed to male privilege. There is no evidence he can offer that cannot be dismissed as evidence of his privileged inability to see clearly.

This is not epistemology. It is a debate-ending mechanism disguised as epistemology. It produces exactly the same outcome as the cult criterion of self-sealing labels that the previous chapter documented: once the label is applied, the labeled person cannot defend themselves without the defense being taken as further evidence of the label's accuracy.

The practical effect on men in institutional settings is documented and consistent. Men who raise concerns about policies that treat them unequally are told their concerns reflect privilege. Men who point out that the data contradicts claims made about male behavior are told their resistance to the data reflects privilege. Men who object to being characterized as inherently dangerous or oppressive are told their objection reflects fragility, which is itself a form of privilege.

A man cannot win inside this framework. That is not a bug. It is the design.

Male Disposability: The Thing Nobody Says Out Loud

There is a concept that the ideological framework around gender does not use as a term of art but that describes something the data documents with precision: male disposability. The idea that male lives and male wellbeing are less socially valued than female lives and female wellbeing, and that this differential valuation is so deeply embedded in cultural assumptions that most people do not notice it.

The data is not ambiguous. Men die at work at roughly eleven times the rate of women. Men constitute roughly ninety-three percent of workplace fatalities. Men are homeless at roughly twice the rate of women. Men are incarcerated at roughly ten times the rate of women. Men die by suicide at four times the rate of women. Men die of every major disease except breast cancer at higher rates than women, and they receive substantially less research funding per death for most of those diseases. Men are the overwhelming majority of combat casualties in every war in human history.

These disparities are not secret. They are documented in public data that anyone can access. What stands out is how little institutional attention they receive compared to comparable disparities affecting women. A gender gap in earnings produces congressional hearings, federal programs, and mandatory corporate reporting requirements. A gender gap in workplace deaths that is eleven times larger receives no equivalent response.

That ideological framework does not explain this asymmetry. It produces it. A framework that defines men as the oppressor class and women as the oppressed class cannot consistently advocate for men's welfare without undermining its own foundational premise. If men are the dominant group, then men's suffering is either invisible, self-inflicted, or evidence of the ways masculine culture harms men themselves, which circles back to toxic masculinity. The framework has no room for the plain observation that men are dying at dramatically higher rates in certain categories and that this matters.

The male disposability concept also explains something that the data on male sacrifice documents across cultures and across history. Every human society has treated male lives as more expendable than female lives in contexts of collective danger, because the mathematics of reproduction favor female survival. Lose half your women and you lose most of your reproductive capacity. Lose half your men and you lose much less. This asymmetry is real, it is ancient, and it shaped the cultural frameworks that assigned men to dangerous roles.

It absorbed the cultural devaluation of male lives that resulted from this historical pattern while at the same time attacking the cultural valorization of male sacrifice that made that devaluation bearable. Men were told that the warrior identity, the protector identity, the provider identity were toxic constructs of patriarchy. They were not told what was supposed to replace those identities as frameworks for making male sacrifice meaningful. The result is men who are still expected to sacrifice but who have been stripped of the cultural language that made sacrifice worth something.

That is a recipe for despair. The suicide data reflects it.

The Privilege of Naming

There is a political science concept called the Overton window: the range of ideas that can be discussed in public without being treated as outside the bounds of acceptable discourse. The language this chapter documents shifted the Overton window for discussions of men and masculinity in ways that systematically disadvantage men in any institutional context where the language is operative.

Inside the framework's vocabulary, certain observations can be made and certain observations cannot. You can observe that men are overrepresented in positions of power and this will be taken as evidence of systemic male advantage. You cannot observe that men are overrepresented among the homeless, the imprisoned, the suicidal, and the workplace-dead without being asked to explain how this is consistent with male privilege, a question designed to exhaust rather than explore.

Vocabulary determines what questions get asked. What questions get asked determines what research gets funded. What research gets funded determines what data gets collected. What data gets collected determines what problems get named. What problems get named determines what solutions get proposed. What solutions get proposed determines whose interests get served.

From vocabulary to policy is not instantaneous. It runs over decades, which is why the Frankfurt School pipeline this book documented in earlier chapters produced its most visible effects not in the generation that was educated in it but in the generation after that. The language shapes what is thinkable.

What is thinkable shapes what is doable. What is doable shapes what gets done.

The language that defines normal male behavior as toxic, that defines male identity as inherently privileged and therefore inherently suspect, that defines male disposability as invisible because the framework cannot see it, has been operative in American educational and corporate institutions for long enough to have shaped the thinking of an entire generation of administrators, policymakers, journalists, and therapists. They did not adopt this language as a deliberate political choice. They absorbed it as the natural vocabulary of their professional formation.

That is how language works when it is successfully deployed as a cultural operation. You do not argue people into using it. You make it the water they swim in. By the time they notice they are swimming, they have already forgotten what it felt like to breathe air.

Microaggressions and the Weaponization of Discomfort

The concept of microaggressions entered academic literature in the 1970s through the work of psychiatrist Chester Pierce, who used it to describe subtle, often unconscious communications of racial hostility. The concept was developed and extended by Derald Wing Sue and colleagues in the 2000s into a framework for identifying and categorizing small-scale insults and indignities experienced by members of marginalized groups.

The microaggression framework has several features that make it a unusually effective tool for the kind of ideological enforcement the previous chapter described. It locates the offense in the receiver's experience rather than the sender's intent. It is not necessary to demonstrate that the person who committed a microaggression meant any harm. It is sufficient that the receiver experienced harm. This moves the standard of evidence from something that can be examined and disputed to something that is definitionally inaccessible to external review.

Applied to male behavior, the microaggression framework functions as follows. A man asks a female colleague a question that she interprets as doubting her competence. Whether the man intended to doubt her competence is irrelevant. Whether the question was about her competence is irrelevant. Whether any reasonable person would have interpreted the question as doubting her competence is irrelevant. Her experience of it as a microaggression is the operative fact, and the organizational response is structured around that experience.

The man in this scenario has no meaningful defense. He cannot appeal to his intent because intent is explicitly excluded. He cannot appeal to the content of the question because the framework holds that microaggressions often operate below the level of explicit content. He cannot appeal to the reasonableness standard because the framework defines the dominant group's sense of what is reasonable as itself a form of privilege. He can confess and commit to doing better, which is the response the framework is designed to produce.

This is not a system for resolving interpersonal conflicts. It is a system for producing confessions. The distinction matters because systems for resolving conflicts aim at truth-finding and the preservation of productive relationships. Systems for producing confessions aim at the consolidation of ideological authority and the demonstration of hierarchy. The microaggression framework in institutional deployment consistently produces the second outcome rather than the first.

The effect on male behavior in institutional settings is exactly what you would predict. Men who have internalized the lesson that their ordinary communications may be experienced as harmful by female colleagues without any failure on their part begin to manage their communications in ways that reduce the risk of accusation. They become less direct. They speak less. They avoid substantive feedback on women's work. They do not mentor women because the mentoring relationship involves the kind of direct, sometimes critical engagement that the microaggression framework defines as potentially harmful.

The organizational research on this pattern is now extensive. The years since the full deployment of the microaggression framework in corporate settings have produced documented declines in male-to-female mentoring relationships, documented increases in men's avoidance of one-on-one professional interactions with women, and documented increases in men's self-censorship in mixed-gender professional settings. These are not the behaviors of men who have learned to treat women as equals. They are the behaviors of men who have learned that women are institutionally dangerous.

That outcome serves nobody. Not the women who lose mentors and honest colleagues. Not the men who lose the ability to function normally in professional settings. Not the organizations that lose the productivity that direct professional engagement produces. The only parties who benefit are those whose institutional power depends on the perpetuation of the framework that produced the outcome.

The Language and the Men It Describes

Step back from the specific terms and consider what the aggregate vocabulary does to the men it describes.

A man who has been processed through the American educational and media system of the past thirty years has been told, in language that his institutions treat as authoritative, that his natural traits are toxic. That his perspective is suspect by virtue of his identity. That his suffering is either invisible or self-inflicted. That his ordinary communications may be harmful without his knowledge or intent. That the masculine identity he developed is a construct that serves oppression. That the sacrifices his sex has made throughout history are not honored values but evidence of a pathological culture.

What does a man do with that?

The data answers the question. Some men accept the framework and spend their lives performing the ideological contrition it demands. Some men reject it entirely and find the rejection validated by online communities that tell them the framework was always a weapon aimed at them. Most men do something more complicated: they disengage. They stop investing in institutions that communicate that they are the problem. They stop forming the civic, professional, and family relationships that institutions are supposed to support. They check out.

The checking out looks different at different socioeconomic levels. An educated man with options may leave a hostile corporate environment and build something independent. A working-class man with fewer options may leave the workforce entirely. A young man without the social resources to manage either path may find his way into the online communities that offer him an alternative identity, some of which are merely countercultural and some of which are genuinely dangerous.

All of these outcomes serve the strategic purpose that the Soviet operation identified in the 1950s. A nation whose men do not believe the institutions are for them is a nation that cannot mobilize those men in defense of those institutions. A nation whose men have been told that their natural traits are pathological is a nation that has degraded its own defensive capacity through its own cultural machinery.

The language built the frame. The frame determined what could be seen. What could not be seen could not be fixed. What could not be fixed accumulated.

The operation that built the payload found a delivery system that the original architects could never have imagined.

Part Three: The Acceleration

The operation found a new delivery mechanism.

It runs twenty-four hours a day on the device in your pocket.

Chapter 7: The Digital Battlefield

The YouTube rabbit hole I described in the Preface was not random. Someone built it.

In January 2017, the United States Senate Intelligence Committee began a formal investigation into Russian interference in American elections. What the investigation documented (published in five volumes between 2019 and 2020) was considerably broader than election interference. It was a systematic account of how the Internet Research Agency used social media platforms to conduct the ideological subversion operation that Yuri Bezmenov had described in 1984, updated for a technological environment that the original architects of the operation could not have imagined.

The scale was industrial. The IRA employed hundreds of people working in shifts around the clock, operating thousands of fake accounts across every major social media platform, producing content designed to amplify every significant social division in American society. The Senate committee documented IRA activity targeting racial conflict, immigration, gun rights, religious identity, and gender relations. On gender relations, the IRA ran accounts on both sides at the same time, feminist accounts and men's rights accounts, producing content designed not to move American opinion in any particular direction but to ensure that men and women on opposite sides of the gender divide would encounter the most extreme possible version of the other side's argument and respond accordingly.

This was not a new operation. It was the same operation Bezmenov described, running through a new delivery mechanism that was several orders of magnitude more efficient than anything the KGB had access to in 1984. The principles were identical. Identify existing divisions. Amplify the most extreme voices on each side. Prevent resolution. Exhaust the society in conflict with itself.

The delivery mechanism had changed everything about the scale at which this was possible.

How the Algorithm Became a Weapon

Social media algorithms are not neutral. They are optimization systems, and what they are optimized for is engagement. Engagement, in the technical definition used by every major platform, means time on platform, clicks, shares, reactions, and comments. The research on what produces maximum engagement is extensive and consistent: outrage produces more engagement than information, fear produces more engagement than reassurance, conflict produces more engagement than resolution, and extreme content produces more engagement than moderate content.

A platform optimized for engagement is therefore a platform optimized for outrage, fear, conflict, and extremity. This is not a conspiracy. It is arithmetic. The engineers who built the engagement optimization systems were not trying to produce a radicalization engine. They were trying to maximize the metric they had been told to maximize. The radicalization was the side effect.

The side effect was well documented internally at every major platform years before it became public knowledge.

Facebook's internal research, portions of which became public through whistleblower Frances Haugen in 2021, showed that the company's own engineers had identified that the recommendation algorithm was driving users toward increasingly extreme content and that the company had chosen not to implement fixes that would have reduced engagement. Instagram's internal research showed that the platform was producing measurable increases in body image problems and depression in teenage girls. YouTube's recommendation algorithm had been shown internally to route users from moderate political content toward increasingly extreme content within a small number of recommendation steps.

The platforms knew. They optimized for engagement anyway because engagement was revenue. The national security implications of running an industrial-scale outrage and radicalization system were not their problem.

Into this system, the IRA and its successors inserted content designed to exploit exactly the dynamics the algorithms were already producing. They did not need to build the radicalization machinery. The platforms had built it. The foreign actors needed only to understand how it worked and feed it the content it was designed to amplify.

The Gender War Goes Online

The conflict between men and women that the Soviet operation had spent decades seeding through universities and media found its ideal amplification environment in social media. Every element that makes gender conflict resistant to resolution in the physical world, the genuine grievances on both sides, the emotional intensity, the difficulty of careful communication across a deeply personal divide, amplified by the algorithmic environment to a degree the original architects of the ideological operation could not have planned for.

The red pill community, the manosphere, the incel forums, the men's rights movement, these online communities did not emerge from nowhere. They emerged from men who had genuine grievances about how they were being treated by institutions, by educational systems, by family courts, by a dating market that the cultural framework documented in this book had systematically distorted. The grievances were real. The communities that formed around them were not created by foreign actors.

What the IRA and its successors did was identify these communities, infiltrate them with accounts, and push their content in the most extreme directions the algorithmic environment would reward. An angry man who joined a men's rights forum because he had been through a damaging divorce was not the IRA's creation. The accounts that told him his experience was evidence of a systematic war against all men, that women were the enemy, that the only rational response was total withdrawal from any relationship with women or with the institutions that had betrayed him, some of those accounts were operated from St. Petersburg.

The Senate Intelligence Committee documented IRA accounts explicitly targeting men's grievances as a vector for social division. The targeting was not ideological in the way Western political discourse usually understands ideology. The IRA did not care whether men became more conservative or more radical or developed any particular political position. It cared that men became angrier, more isolated, more convinced that the system was irredeemably hostile to them, and less capable of forming the social bonds that would have made them resilient.

Resilient men are hard to radicalize and hard to recruit. Isolated, angry men with no social anchors are easy. The operation understood this. Social media made it operational at scale.

TikTok: The Chinese Improvement

Russia used social media to amplify existing divisions. China built the platform.

TikTok is owned by ByteDance, a Chinese company. ByteDance is subject to Chinese law, including the National Intelligence Law of 2017, which requires Chinese companies to support and cooperate with national intelligence work. The app operates under different algorithmic rules in China, where it exists as Douyin, than in the rest of the world, where it operates as TikTok. This is not speculation. It is documented by researchers who have run controlled comparisons of content served to users in each market.

The comparison lands hard. A new account created in China and fed a diet of short videos receives content promoting patriotism, scientific achievement, historical accomplishment, and cultural pride. A new account created in the United States and fed a short video diet receives content optimized for emotional arousal and social conflict, with heavy representation of content about racial grievance, gender conflict, body image, and political polarization. The difference is not random. It reflects deliberate algorithmic choices that serve one government's strategic interests.

Gender content served to American users skews in measurable ways. Research comparing TikTok content served to American users against content served through comparable platforms shows that TikTok over-indexes on content that promotes conflict between men and women, content that presents male-female relationships as inherently adversarial, and content that presents traditional masculinity as dangerous. The algorithm promotes this content because it produces the engagement metrics the algorithm is optimizing for. Whether the specific content decisions that produce this outcome are deliberate policy choices of the Chinese government or emergent properties of an engagement-optimization system operating under Chinese law is a question the available evidence does not definitively resolve. What the evidence does establish is the outcome: the content environment served to American young men is measurably different from the content environment served to Chinese young men on the same company's platform, and the difference consistently serves Chinese strategic interests.

Young men who spend hours on TikTok consuming content about why women are hypergamous, why traditional relationships are traps, why the system is rigged against them, are not consuming this content because TikTok has identified their interests and served them. They are consuming it because TikTok's algorithm has determined that this content produces maximum engagement from their demographic and because the government that oversees TikTok benefits from American men being angry, isolated, and distrustful of American institutions.

This is not a theory. It is the documented output of a system whose operational logic is visible in the data. The men consuming the content are real. The grievances the content exploits are real. The foreign hand feeding those grievances into a system optimized to amplify them is also real, and it is not operating in anyone's interest but its own.

The Domestic Amplification Machine

Foreign actors did not build the digital gender war alone. They had substantial domestic help from an attention economy that found gender conflict to be among the most reliably engaging content categories available.

Content creators on every platform discovered that videos about gender conflict (whether feminist content about male behavior or manosphere content about female behavior) produced dramatically higher engagement than comparable content on almost any other topic. The emotional intensity of the subject, the universal personal relevance, and the way the algorithmic environment rewards outrage over nuance produced a content ecosystem in which the most extreme voices on both sides were the most financially rewarded.

A creator who made measured, accurate observations about the genuine challenges facing men in contemporary America might accumulate a modest audience. A creator who told men that women were their enemies and that the entire system was designed to destroy them could build a million-person following and monetize it through merchandise, premium content, and speaking fees. The attention economy created financial incentives for the most divisive possible framing of every gender question, and those incentives operated on domestic creators independently of any foreign influence operation.

The result was a content ecosystem in which the algorithmic amplification of foreign influence operations and the financial incentives of the domestic attention economy converged on the same target. Both systems were optimized for the same output: maximum conflict, minimum resolution, endless engagement. The foreign actors provided strategic intent. The domestic creators provided real grievance. The platforms provided the amplification infrastructure. The young men consuming the content provided the attention that made the whole system financially viable.

Each element of this system would have been less effective without the others. Together they produced something that none of them could have produced independently: a generation of young men whose primary framework for understanding gender relations was constructed in an environment optimized to produce the most adversarial possible version of that framework.

What the Data Shows About the Damage

The measurable effects of the digital gender war on young men's attitudes, mental health, and behavior are now extensive enough to constitute a research literature rather than isolated findings.

Young men between eighteen and thirty who report heavy social media use, especially heavy use of platforms with algorithm-driven content feeds, show measurably higher rates of negative attitudes toward women, higher rates of endorsement of adversarial gender frameworks, higher rates of social isolation, and higher rates of depression and anxiety than comparable young men with lower social media use. The correlation is solid across multiple studies and multiple countries.

The direction of causation is contested, as it always is in social media research. Men who already hold negative views about women may be more likely to seek out content that confirms those views. But the experimental research on algorithmic radicalization (studies that track content consumption over time in controlled conditions) consistently shows that the algorithm moves users toward more extreme positions regardless of their starting point. You do not need to begin with negative views about women to end up in content environments that promote them. You need only to begin using a platform optimized for engagement.

The dating and relationship data compounds the attitudinal data. Young men in the current cohort are forming romantic relationships at dramatically lower rates than any previous cohort in the recorded data. The percentage of men under thirty who report having had no sexual partner in the previous year has been rising since roughly 2008, which is approximately when smartphone adoption and social media use became widespread among that age group. The correlation is not proof of causation but it is consistent with every other piece of the picture.

Young men who have spent their formative years in a content environment that presents women as adversaries, relationships as traps, and vulnerability as weakness are not well-prepared to form the relationships that human development requires. The loneliness and isolation that result feed back into the content consumption patterns that produced the attitudes in the first place. The algorithm has no incentive to break that cycle. It is optimized to perpetuate it.

The Counter-Radicalization Problem

The people who run counter-extremism programs in government and in civil society have spent years working on the problem of online radicalization toward violent political extremism. The frameworks they have developed work reasonably well for the specific problem of people being recruited into organizations that use violence to pursue political goals. They do not work well for the diffuse, algorithm-driven radicalization of a generation of young men toward a worldview that is hostile to women and to institutions without being organized around any specific political or violent program.

You cannot deradicalize someone from an algorithm. There is no organization to leave, no leader to denounce, no ideology that can be countered with a competing ideology. There is only a content environment that has shaped a framework for understanding the world, reinforced by every social connection the person has made inside that environment, and economically sustained by an attention economy that has no incentive to change it.

The foreign actors who seeded and amplified this environment understood this when they chose social media as their delivery mechanism. A pamphlet can be countered with another pamphlet. A broadcast can be countered with another broadcast. An algorithm optimized for outrage cannot be countered with content that promotes nuance, because nuance does not produce the engagement metrics that determine what gets distributed.

The men who have been shaped by this environment are not stupid. Many of them are perceptive about the genuine failures of the institutions and the genuine ways the cultural framework documented in this book has disadvantaged them. Their analysis of what happened to them is not wrong. What was done to their analysis is wrong: it was taken by an environment designed to produce maximum anger and minimum resolution, and processed through that environment until what came out the other side was a framework that made constructive response impossible.

An angry man who understands that the educational system failed him has something to work with. An angry man who has been told that women are the enemy, that any relationship with a woman is capitulation to an adversarial force, that the only rational response to a hostile world is withdrawal, that man has been disarmed. Not by the truth of his grievances but by what the digital environment did to those grievances in the processing.

The Strategic Picture

Pull back to the level of strategic analysis and the digital battlefield looks like this.

The Soviet cultural operation seeded an ideology in American universities beginning in the 1960s. The ideology spread through American institutions over three generations, producing the educational failures, the language framework, and the institutional hostility to masculinity documented in the preceding chapters. By the 2010s, the damage was real and measurable, and the men experiencing it had genuine grievances.

Social media, and the algorithmically optimized content delivery systems built by American technology companies, created an environment in which those grievances could be identified, aggregated, and amplified at industrial scale. The domestic attention economy created financial incentives for the most adversarial possible framing of those grievances. Russian active measures through the IRA inserted content designed to push the most extreme versions of that adversarial framing. The Chinese government built and operates a platform structured to maximize the engagement of young Americans with content that serves Chinese strategic interests, including content that promotes gender conflict and institutional distrust.

The operation that Bezmenov described in 1984 as requiring fifteen to twenty years per generation because that was the speed of institutional education now operates in something approaching real time. A piece of content produced in St. Petersburg or designed by a ByteDance algorithm can reach a million young American men within twenty-four hours. The feedback loop between content production and audience response that used to require years of institutional development now closes in days.

The men on the receiving end of this operation did not choose it. They were born into a world where the institutions that were supposed to prepare them for adult life had been compromised by sixty years of ideological capture, where the hormonal environment had been altered by sixty years of unmonitored chemical change, where the educational system had spent thirteen years treating their natural behavior as pathological, and where the digital environment that dominated their social development was a radicalization engine operated for the benefit of foreign actors and domestic profit motives with no stake in their wellbeing.

That is not a description of personal failure. It is a description of an operation.

The operation did not need the institutions to fall. It needed them to stay standing while becoming something else.

Chapter 8: The Institutions Fall

I watched this happen in the professional world I worked in. Not a sudden collapse. A slow substitution of one set of assumptions for another, until the institution I was looking at was not the institution I had known.

Institutions do not collapse all at once. They hollow out. The walls stand, the signage remains, the organizational charts are updated and redistributed, and from the outside everything looks more or less intact. What has changed is what happens inside. The people who run the institution begin making decisions according to a different set of priorities than the institution was built to serve. The mission gets redefined, or subordinated, or quietly abandoned in favor of something that produces less friction with the framework the institution has absorbed. The institutional shell persists long after the institutional function has been compromised.

This chapter documents what happened to four institutions that were central to America's capacity to defend itself and sustain itself: the military, the corporation, the family, and the church. All four absorbed the ideological framework documented in the preceding chapters. All four show measurable degradation in the functions they were built to perform. None of them collapsed dramatically. All of them hollowed out in ways that are now visible in the data.

The military recruitment crisis. The DEI apparatus in American corporations. The marriage and birth rate collapse. The emptying of the pews. Each of these is a story about an institution that was supposed to hold when other things gave way and that found itself instead absorbing the same framework that was producing the failures it was supposed to counteract.

The Military: When the Warrior Culture Broke

In 2022, the United States Army missed its recruiting goal by fifteen thousand soldiers, roughly twenty-five percent of its target. It was the Army's worst recruiting year since the establishment of the all-volunteer force in 1973. The Navy, the Air Force, and the Marine Corps all missed their targets in the same year. The following year was not meaningfully better. The military had a recruiting crisis, and the military knew it, and the military's own internal research on the cause produced findings that the institutional culture made it nearly impossible to act on.

I find this disgusting. Not at the young men. At what produced them. The country has always had trouble filling its military in peacetime. It was hard to get recruits until Pearl Harbor. But that was a different kind of problem. This is not apathy in a country at peace. This is a country that has so thoroughly degraded its own young men that too many of them cannot serve even if they wanted to.

The population of young Americans who meet the military's basic eligibility requirements has been shrinking for reasons that track everything documented in this book. Physical fitness standards are met by a declining percentage of young men. Educational requirements are met by a declining percentage of young men. Drug test requirements are met by a declining percentage of young men. Criminal record exclusions affect a rising percentage of young men. The pipeline from which the military draws its recruits has been degraded by the same forces that degraded it everywhere else.

But the physical eligibility problem is not the whole story. The military's own research found that among young men who were physically and legally eligible to serve, propensity to enlist had been declining for years. Eligible young men were choosing not to serve at increasing rates. When the research drilled into why, it found answers that military leadership found uncomfortable: young men did not believe the military was an institution that respected them or valued what they had to offer.

I hired veterans. At least one of them left his next posting partly because of this. He did not use that language. But when he described what changed, that is what he was describing.

The military's effort to address its diversity, equity, and inclusion gaps over the preceding decade had produced training programs, promotional materials, and institutional messaging that young men interpreted as communicating that traditional military virtues (toughness, aggression, willingness to fight) were not valued or were actively problematic. Recruiting campaigns that featured soldiers doing yoga and discussing their feelings and working through family conflicts produced mockery rather than enlistment. The young men who were most likely to enlist, young men from military families, young men who had grown up with a martial identity, young men who saw military service as an expression of masculine virtue, looked at those campaigns and concluded that the military had become something other than what their fathers had served in.

They were not wrong. The military had absorbed the ideological framework. Mandatory diversity training. Investigations of social media posts for ideological compliance. Promotion processes that explicitly weighted demographic factors. A senior officer corps that had learned to signal ideological alignment as a prerequisite for advancement. The institution that exists to project lethal force in defense of national interests had incorporated the assumption that expressions of traditional military culture might be harmful and required management.

Military leadership has documented the operational consequences. does not discuss publicly but that appear in classified assessments, congressional testimony, and the research of military sociologists who study unit cohesion and combat effectiveness. An institution whose members have been trained to second-guess whether their natural aggressive instincts are problematic is an institution that has degraded its own combat effectiveness. An institution that has made ideological performance a prerequisite for advancement has selected against the blunt, direct, results-oriented leadership style that military operations require and selected for the politically sophisticated, careful, self-monitoring leadership style that institutional survival in ideologically charged environments rewards.

What emerges from this process is not the same military that the nation's security requires. It is a military that looks like the same military from the outside while being functionally compromised in ways that will not become fully visible until the next serious test.

The Corporation: When DEI Became the Mission

From approximately 2012, the American corporation spent roughly a decade, to 2022, systematically incorporating the ideological framework into its operations at every level. Diversity, equity, and inclusion departments were created, staffed, and given organizational authority. Mandatory training programs were implemented. Hiring processes were restructured to weight demographic factors. Performance management systems were modified to incorporate ideological compliance as a dimension of professional effectiveness. The entire apparatus of the Frankfurt School pipeline, delivered through corporate HR infrastructure rather than university administration, was deployed across the American private sector at a scale that dwarfed its university origins.

It cost billions. Nobody checked if it worked.

Nobody ever rigorously established a business case for this apparatus. The research on diversity and business performance is mixed at best and was consistently overstated in the corporate communications that promoted DEI initiatives. The McKinsey reports on diversity and profitability that circulated through boardrooms in this period have been subjected to serious methodological criticism that received far less attention than the original reports. The causal claims (that diverse teams perform better, that DEI initiatives improve financial outcomes) rest on correlational data that cannot establish the direction of causation and that does not hold up across the full body of research.

What the corporation discovered, slowly and then with increasing speed after approximately 2022, was that the DEI apparatus had costs that were not reflected in the business case presentations. Productivity losses from mandatory training programs that took skilled employees away from productive work. Legal liability from employment decisions made on demographic grounds that exposed companies to discrimination claims from white and Asian male employees who could document that they had been passed over for less qualified candidates. Morale degradation among employees who experienced the mandatory ideological training as coercive and who responded by reducing their discretionary effort. Senior talent departures, predominantly male, as experienced professionals concluded that institutions that had defined their identity as inherently suspect were not institutions worth continuing to invest in.

The rollback that began around 2023 was rapid by the standards of institutional change. Major corporations that had built elaborate DEI infrastructures began dismantling them. The chief diversity officers who had been hired in large numbers began losing their jobs. The mandatory training programs began being quietly retired. The public commitments that had been made in the aftermath of 2020's social justice moment were walked back in the language of operational efficiency.

The experiment was over. The results were in.

What the rollback revealed was that the DEI apparatus had served the ideological framework's institutional interests far more than it had served the corporations that implemented it. The corporations had absorbed the framework because the social and reputational cost of not absorbing it had been high during the period when the framework's cultural authority was at its peak. When that authority began to erode, the corporations shed the apparatus with a speed that demonstrated how little genuine conviction had underwritten the adoption.

Men who had been managed out, passed over, and trained to regard their natural professional behaviors as problematic during this period do not get those years back. The institutional culture that was built around their management does not disappear when the training program is cancelled. The assumptions embed themselves in the people who were formed by them and persist in institutional behavior long after the formal apparatus is gone.

The Family: The Institutional Foundation That Crumbled

Family is not usually described as an institution in the same register as the military or the corporation. It is the institution that all the others depend on: the unit that produces the next generation, transmits the values and skills that make citizens capable of self-governance, provides the primary social support network that keeps people from requiring institutional intervention, and generates the civic commitment that makes collective defense possible.

This is the part that makes me sad more than angry. What we spent generations building is in slow decline. Not because people stopped wanting families. Because the conditions that produce families have been systematically dismantled. And the people paying the highest price are young people who will never know what they missed: the children they did not have, the marriages that did not happen, the families that did not form. We are looking at a demographic hole that will take a hundred years to fill. Maybe longer.

American family structure has been in measurable statistical decline since the 1960s. Marriage rates have been falling for sixty years. Birth rates have been falling for sixty years. Divorce rates rose through the 1970s and have remained elevated. The percentage of children born outside of marriage has risen from roughly five percent in 1960 to over forty percent today. The percentage of children growing up without a father in the household has risen correspondingly. None of these trends reversed during the period when the ideological framework was most institutionally dominant. All of them worsened.

Causation is not simple.t simple and it runs in multiple directions. The framework did not cause the economic changes that made single-income family formation difficult. It did not cause the pill, though as the chapter on the chemical attack documented, the pill interacted with the framework in ways that neither produced independently. The framework did contribute to the cultural shifts that reduced the social and institutional support for marriage as an expectation rather than an option, that redefined male commitment as a form of female constraint rather than a form of male investment in something larger than himself, and that produced the legal environment around divorce and child custody that rational men now factor into their decision about whether to marry at all.

The men who are not marrying are not doing so because they are lazy or because they lack drive. The research on why young men are not forming families produces consistent findings: they do not believe the institutional environment around marriage protects them adequately. They have watched fathers lose their children, their homes, and significant portions of their future income in divorce proceedings that the family court system handles in ways that consistently disadvantage men. They have absorbed the cultural message that commitment makes them vulnerable and that vulnerability is dangerous. They have looked at the risk-reward calculation that marriage presents and concluded that the risks are too high.

That calculation is not irrational given the environment. A man who commits to a marriage in the current legal and cultural environment is making a significant economic bet with limited downside protection, in a cultural context that has redefined his natural role as protector and provider as an assertion of patriarchal dominance, in an institutional context where the divorce and custody system will most likely award primary custody to his wife if the marriage ends. The men opting out of this arrangement are responding rationally to an institutional environment that has been made hostile to their participation.

The children who are not being born as a result are the long-term cost. The birth rate in the United States fell below replacement level in 2011 and has not recovered. The societies with the lowest birth rates in the world are the societies where the ideological framework documented in this book has been most completely implemented: South Korea, Japan, parts of northern and western Europe. The correlation is not perfect and the causation is not simple, but the pattern is consistent enough to require explanation. The framework that defined traditional family formation as patriarchal oppression produced populations that are not replacing themselves.

The Church: When the Transcendent Framework Emptied

American religious attendance has been declining for fifty years. The percentage of Americans who identify as religiously unaffiliated has risen from roughly five percent in the 1970s to over thirty percent today. The speed of the decline accelerated in the 2000s and 2010s, with young adults and men leading the decline.

Men leave religious institutions at higher rates than women and always have. The reasons are complex and predate the ideological framework documented in this book. But the specific pattern of male departure from religious institutions over the past four decades tracks the penetration of the ideological framework into those institutions with a consistency that suggests more than coincidence.

I watched this happen over years, through the articles and videos that tracked what these institutions were doing to themselves. It was not sudden. It was a slow substitution, and by the time it was visible to everyone, it was too late for most of them.

The mainline Protestant denominations that most fully incorporated the ideological framework into their theology and practice, the ones that adopted gender-neutral liturgy, that replaced the language of sin and redemption with the language of social justice, that restructured their institutional priorities around the framework's preferred causes, experienced the fastest and most complete male departure. The denominations that maintained traditional theological frameworks and traditional expectations for male behavior and male responsibility experienced slower decline and in some cases growth.

This pattern is not surprising if you understand what religious institutions provided to men that the ideological framework cannot provide. Religious institutions gave men a framework for understanding their sacrifices as meaningful, a community that honored rather than pathologized their protective instincts, a set of expectations that treated male commitment as virtue rather than oppression, and a transcendent account of why any of it mattered. The ideological framework offers men none of these things. It offers them instead an account of themselves as the historical source of oppression, a demand for ongoing confession and amendment, and a social position that is permanently provisional because the framework's criteria for male acceptability can always be tightened.

I know men like this. The missing element is hard to spot until you look into their eyes and their lives. They have explanations for everything. They have reasons. But there is something not there. The relationship with something larger than themselves, call it God or faith or whatever you want, and it is suppressed or gone, and they make excuses for why they do not miss it, and you can see in how they live that they do.

Men who have internalized the ideological framework and men who have left religious institutions for secular lives have not necessarily found replacements for what those institutions provided. The data on male social isolation, on the decline of male friendship and civic participation, on the rise of male loneliness as a documented public health concern, reflects in part the loss of the institutional frameworks that organized male social life and gave it meaning.

The gym replaced the church for some men. The online community replaced the civic organization for others. The podcast replaced the sermon for others still. None of these replacements provide what the institutions they replaced provided: intergenerational transmission of values, accountability to a community that knows you over time, the experience of being part of something larger than your individual gratification, and a framework for understanding suffering and sacrifice as meaningful rather than merely painful.

The Pattern in the Rubble

Look at all four institutions together and the pattern is the same. Each institution absorbed the ideological framework. Each institution experienced measurable degradation in the functions it was built to perform. Each institution's degradation compounded the degradation of the others, because the institutions were interdependent in ways that became visible only when they began failing at the same time.

The military needs men who were raised in intact families by fathers who transmitted the values of service, sacrifice, and physical courage. When the family produces fewer such men, the military's recruiting pool degrades. The corporation needs men who were educated in institutions that built competence and confidence. When the educational system produces men who lack those qualities, the corporation's talent pool degrades. The family needs men who believe that commitment and sacrifice are meaningful. When the cultural framework tells men that their natural protective instincts are pathological and when the church that once gave those instincts a transcendent framework has been emptied, men do not form families.

The institutions were supposed to be mutually reinforcing. The family produced citizens for the military and workers for the corporation and congregants for the church. The military produced the civic commitment that made democratic governance viable. The corporation produced the prosperity that made family formation economically feasible. The church produced the values framework that made all the others cohere. When all four absorbed the same framework at the same time, the mutual reinforcement became mutual degradation.

If you are reading this and you recognize yourself in any of it: get help. Get out of the house. Find social groups that are doing something real. Get involved with your community. Get out of your echo chamber. The online world that is feeding you content about how everything is rigged and women are the enemy and there is no point in trying. It is designed to keep you there. It is the operation working on you right now. Put the phone down.

This is what a successful ideological subversion operation looks like from the inside. Not a dramatic collapse. A slow hollowing. The institutions stand. The men who were supposed to fill them and be shaped by them and defend them are somewhere else, in their parents' basements, in online communities, in the workforce participation statistics as absences rather than presences, in the suicide data, in the recruiting shortfalls, in the birth rate, in the empty pews.

The operation did not need to destroy the institutions. It needed to make the institutions inhospitable to the men who would have sustained them. The institutions did the rest themselves, faithfully implementing a framework that guaranteed their own hollowing, each one convinced until recently that it was doing the right thing.

Every institution that was supposed to resist has become, in some measure, a vehicle for what it was supposed to resist.

Part Four: The Cost

What the operation produced.

In numbers. Not opinions. Numbers.

Chapter 9: The Data

Arguments can be dismissed. Data is harder.

Everything in this book to this point has been argument: a case built from documented history, academic research, strategic analysis, and institutional observation. Arguments can always be countered with other arguments. The person who does not want to see what this book is showing can find reasons to dispute the framing, question the sources, or simply decline to follow the reasoning to its conclusion.

This chapter is different. This chapter is numbers. Specific, sourced, publicly available numbers from government databases, peer-reviewed research, and international comparative data. The numbers do not argue. They report. What they report is a picture of American male decline so consistent across so many independent data categories that the accumulated weight of it is difficult to dismiss regardless of how strongly you resist the explanation this book has offered for why it happened.

Look at the numbers. Then decide what you think caused them.

Education

College enrollment: Women now constitute approximately sixty percent of college students in the United States. Men constitute forty percent. The gap has been widening continuously since the early 1980s. At the current rate of change, the ratio will reach two women for every one man enrolled in college within the next decade.

College completion: The gap in completion rates exceeds the gap in enrollment rates. Women who enroll in college complete degrees at higher rates than men. The combination of lower enrollment and lower completion means that the number of college-educated women now substantially exceeds the number of college-educated men in every age cohort under forty.

Reading proficiency: The National Assessment of Educational Progress, the standardized test administered to American students nationwide, has shown a consistent and widening gap between male and female reading proficiency at every tested grade level for the entirety of its existence. At the fourth-grade level, the gap has been present and measurable since the test was first administered in 1971. It has never closed. It has widened.

High school graduation: Male high school graduation rates lag female graduation rates by approximately five percentage points nationally. The gap is larger in lower-income communities and in communities with weaker educational infrastructure.

Special education: Boys are identified for special education services at approximately twice the rate of girls. Boys are diagnosed with attention deficit disorder and prescribed stimulant medication at approximately four times the rate of girls. These ratios have been consistent and widening since the 1990s.

Graduate and professional education: Women now earn the majority of master's degrees, the majority of doctoral degrees outside of engineering and computer science, and the majority of law degrees and medical degrees. The professional credential pipeline that feeds the leadership of American institutions is now majority female in every category except the hard sciences and engineering.

Work

Labor force participation: Prime-age male labor force participation, defined as men between twenty-five and fifty-four years old either working or actively seeking work, has declined from approximately ninety-seven percent in the mid-1950s to approximately eighty-six percent in 2024. Approximately seven million prime-age American men are currently outside the labor force, neither working nor looking for work. They are not counted in unemployment statistics. They do not appear in the headline numbers. They are simply gone from the economic life of the country.

The seven million number requires context. These are not men between jobs. They are not men on temporary leave. These are men who have permanently exited the labor market. Bureau of Labor Statistics research on this population finds that the majority report spending their time in leisure activities, primarily video games and online media consumption. A substantial minority report chronic pain or disability. A small percentage report caregiving responsibilities. Almost none are pursuing education or training. They have stopped.

Wage trends: The inflation-adjusted wages of men without college degrees have been declining since the early 1970s. The manufacturing and industrial jobs that provided the primary employment base for working-class men in the post-war period have largely disappeared. The jobs that replaced them pay less, offer less stability, confer less social status, and provide less of the structured male community that the old industrial workplace provided alongside the paycheck.

Occupational concentration: Men and women have always worked in different occupational concentrations. What has changed over the past forty years is the relative social valuation of those concentrations. The occupations that are majority-male (construction, manufacturing, transportation, extraction) have declined in both absolute numbers and social prestige. The occupations that are majority-female (education, healthcare, social services, administration) have grown in both absolute numbers and social prestige. The culture that once honored the man who built things with his hands now barely notices him.

Entrepreneurship: Male entrepreneurship rates have been declining for decades. The businesses men start are smaller, less well-funded, and less likely to survive their first five years than they were a generation ago. The institutional infrastructure around entrepreneurship (bank lending, angel investment, venture capital) has shifted in ways that disadvantage the kinds of businesses that male entrepreneurs traditionally built.

Health

Life expectancy gap: American men die on average approximately six years earlier than American women. This gap has been widening. In 1920, the life expectancy gap was approximately one year. The current gap is the largest it has been in recorded American history. The widening is not primarily driven by cardiovascular disease or cancer, the traditional male killers. It is driven by what public health researchers call deaths of despair: suicide, drug overdose, and alcohol-related liver disease.

Suicide: American men die by suicide at four times the rate of American women. Suicide is the leading cause of death for men between the ages of ten and forty-four. The rate has been rising for thirty years. The rise is steepest among middle-aged men without college degrees, the demographic that has experienced the most complete combination of economic displacement, cultural marginalization, and institutional abandonment documented in this book.

Drug overdose: Men die of drug overdoses at approximately twice the rate of women. The opioid crisis, which killed more than eighty thousand Americans in 2021, is disproportionately a male crisis. The communities where overdose deaths are concentrated are disproportionately the communities where manufacturing employment collapsed and where the ideological framework that might have offered an alternative identity never arrived because those communities never adopted it.

Mental health: Men are diagnosed with depression at approximately half the rate of women, which mental health researchers consistently identify as evidence of underdiagnosis rather than better male mental health outcomes. Men are less likely to seek mental health treatment, less likely to have social support networks that would prompt them to seek treatment, and less likely to be in environments that recognize male distress as distress rather than as personal failure or social dysfunction.

Testosterone: As documented in Chapter 4, male testosterone levels in the United States have been declining at approximately one percent per year for several decades. A thirty-year-old man today has testosterone levels approximately thirty percent lower than a thirty-year-old man in 1990. The clinical threshold for testosterone deficiency in American men has been adjusted downward multiple times, effectively redefining normal male hormonal function to accommodate a population-wide decline rather than treating the decline as a public health problem requiring response.

Physical fitness: Approximately seventy-seven percent of young Americans between seventeen and twenty-four are ineligible to serve in the military for medical, physical fitness, or drug-related reasons. The physical fitness disqualification component of that number has been growing. The young American male body is, by the standards of previous generations and by the standards of military readiness, in measurably worse condition than it was fifty years ago.

Family and Demographics

Marriage rate: The marriage rate in the United States has fallen by more than fifty percent since 1970. Americans are marrying later, marrying less frequently, and divorcing more frequently than at any point in the country's history. The decline is steepest among men without college degrees, who have experienced the most complete combination of factors this book documents.

Birth rate: The total fertility rate in the United States fell below the replacement level of 2.1 children per woman in 2011 and has continued to decline. The 2023 total fertility rate was approximately 1.62, the lowest recorded in American history. The United States is now, on demographic trajectory, a shrinking society. The workforce required to sustain the Social Security and Medicare obligations that current policy has made is not going to exist.

Father absence: Approximately forty percent of American children are born to unmarried mothers. Approximately twenty-three percent of American children live in households with no father present. The research on outcomes for children raised without fathers is extensive and consistent across decades and across methodological approaches: children raised without fathers show higher rates of poverty, lower academic achievement, higher rates of behavioral problems, higher rates of involvement with the criminal justice system, and lower rates of stable adult family formation. The fatherlessness crisis produces the next generation's crisis, compounded.

Loneliness: A 2023 survey by the Survey Center on American Life found that the percentage of men reporting having no close friends had increased from three percent in 1990 to fifteen percent in 2023. Men report smaller social networks, less frequent contact with friends, and lower satisfaction with their social relationships than at any point in the survey history. The rise in male loneliness predates the pandemic and accelerated during it. Male loneliness is now recognized as a public health crisis by the U.S. Surgeon General, who issued an advisory on loneliness in 2023 that explicitly identified men and boys as high-risk groups.

Criminal Justice

Incarceration: Men constitute approximately ninety-three percent of the American prison population. The United States incarcerates more people than any country on earth, and the overwhelming majority of those people are men. This disparity is so large and so persistent that it barely registers in public discourse about criminal justice, which focuses instead on racial disparities in incarceration (which are real and significant) while treating the gender disparity as so natural as to require no explanation.

Court outcomes: Men receive longer sentences than women for equivalent offenses at every level of the criminal justice system. The sentencing gap between men and women is larger than the sentencing gap between racial groups that receives far more institutional attention. Men are less likely to receive probation instead of incarceration for equivalent offenses. Men are less likely to have their charges reduced through plea bargaining. The criminal justice system treats men and women differently at every decision point, and the difference consistently disadvantages men.

Homicide: Men are the victims of approximately eighty percent of homicides in the United States. Men are also the perpetrators of approximately ninety percent of homicides. The male homicide victimization rate receives almost no institutional attention as a men's issue. The male perpetration rate receives substantial institutional attention, primarily through the lens of toxic masculinity and the pathologization of male aggression.

The International Comparison

If the trends documented in this chapter were the product of universal modernization (inevitable consequences of economic development and social progress that any advanced society would experience) they would appear uniformly across all advanced societies. They do not.

Russia: Russian male life expectancy is approximately sixty-seven years, compared to seventy-six years for American men. Russian male suicide rates are among the highest in the world. Russia has a severe demographic crisis driven by male mortality and low birth rates. The data suggests that the cultural and ideological attack on American masculinity documented in this book did not immunize Russia from the consequences of male social collapse. It exported a mechanism of collapse while experiencing a different version of the same collapse domestically.

China: China has a birth rate even lower than the United States, driven in part by the legacy of the one-child policy and in part by the economic pressures that make family formation difficult for young Chinese men. The young men who cannot afford to marry in China's housing-price-inflated economy are called "lying flat", a phrase that means the same thing as the American concept of men checking out. The Chinese government is alarmed by this trend and has implemented policies designed to reverse it, including the promotion of traditional masculine virtues in Chinese youth content, the same content that Chinese platforms serve Chinese youth while serving American youth the adversarial gender content documented in Chapter 7.

South Korea and Japan: Both countries have birth rates significantly below the United States, at approximately 0.72 and 1.20 respectively as of recent measurements. Both countries have implemented the gender ideology framework more completely than most Western countries in their educational and corporate institutions. Both countries have severe problems with male social withdrawal, documented in the hikikomori phenomenon in Japan and comparable patterns in South Korea. Both countries have governments that are alarmed by the demographic trajectory and have spent billions attempting to reverse it with no meaningful success.

The Outliers: Countries that have maintained higher birth rates and stronger male civic and economic participation tend to share characteristics that are almost the inverse of the countries with the worst outcomes: strong religious institutional life, less complete penetration of the ideological framework into educational and corporate institutions, cultural frameworks that honor rather than pathologize traditional male roles, and lower rates of social media use among young men. Israel, with a birth rate above replacement and strong military service rates, is the most prominent example among developed countries. The Israeli case is complicated by religious and demographic factors that make direct comparison difficult, but the pattern is consistent with the broader picture.

What the Numbers Add Up To

Read the data categories together and what you see is not a collection of separate problems requiring separate solutions. What you see is a single system-level failure expressing itself through multiple indicators at the same time.

Boys falling behind in school becomes men falling out of the workforce becomes men not marrying becomes children not being born becomes military not recruiting becomes institutions not being sustained becomes a civilization not replacing itself. Each link in the chain follows from the previous one. The chain began with the decision documented in Chapter 1 and accelerated through everything documented in the chapters that followed.

The numbers are not a judgment on the men they describe. The men who are not working, not marrying, not serving, not showing up are responding rationally to an environment that was systematically shaped to produce exactly these responses. A man who was failed by his educational system, told his natural traits were pathological, watched his father destroyed in a divorce proceeding, consumed ten thousand hours of content designed to make him distrust women and institutions, and found that the institutions that survived offered him no honored place, that man's withdrawal is not a character flaw. It is a rational response to a strategic operation that targeted him.

Understanding that changes what the numbers mean. They are not a measure of male failure. They are a measure of how much damage a well-designed and well-executed ideological operation can produce over sixty years when it targets the right pressure points in the right sequence.

There is one more thing the data reveals that deserves its own paragraph. The institutions and academic departments most responsible for delivering the ideological framework documented in this book are the same institutions with the least satisfying answers for what the data shows. Gender studies departments cannot explain the male education gap in terms their own framework does not produce. HR departments that ran diversity training for a decade cannot account for the male mentorship collapse their own programs generated. The people who most confidently defended the framework are the people least able to explain its outcomes. That is not a coincidence. A framework that defines male underperformance as evidence of systemic male advantage, and male withdrawal as evidence of male fragility, has built its own immunity to the data that refutes it. The data does not care. It accumulates regardless.

The next chapter asks the question that the numbers make unavoidable: who benefits from all of this, and what does that comparison look like when you put American numbers next to the numbers of the countries that designed the operation?

Interlude: Seven People

The preceding chapter is numbers. This is what the numbers look like when they have faces.

None of what follows is composite or invented. These are documented public accounts of real people, drawn from court records, congressional testimony, published interviews, and on-the-record journalism. They are here because the argument of this book is about what happens to specific human beings, not to demographic categories, and because data without people is just arithmetic.

Five of these accounts are men. Two are women. Both sexes are in the data. Both sexes are paying the cost.

Jihad Miller, Age Six. Baltimore County Public Schools.

David Miller is a father of three boys who went through the Baltimore County public school system. His middle son Jihad was diagnosed with ADHD and apraxia, a condition that made it difficult for him to speak. In 2025, Miller described what school looked like for Jihad in an NPR interview.

Every day Miller came to pick up his son, the report was the same. Jihad had a sad face. He wasn't listening. He was in timeout. He was in the corner, in tears. Miller said it wasn't good for his self-esteem at a very young age to always be told that you're doing something wrong at six.

Think about what that means accumulated over years. A boy who is told daily, from the moment he enters the institution that is supposed to build him, that his natural way of being is wrong. Not redirected. Not channeled. Wrong. The data shows boys are suspended at more than twice the rate of girls and medicated at four times the rate. Jihad Miller is not an outlier. He is the ratio, with a name and a face and a father watching it happen.

David Miller did not want his son treated as gifted or exceptional. He wanted him treated like a boy. Like a child whose energy and difficulty sitting still and trouble with emotional regulation were developmental phases to be worked with, not diagnoses to be managed. That is not a high bar. It is the bar the current system consistently fails to clear.

What Jihad Miller carries out of those early years, the self-concept formed in the corner with the sad face, is not visible in any dataset. It shapes what he believes about himself in every institution he enters for the rest of his life.

Craig Mallory, Age 52. Communications Executive. Charlotte, North Carolina.

Craig Mallory spent years building a career in healthcare communications. By 2018 he was the head of communications and marketing at Novant Health, a major hospital system, with a documented record of strong performance and no history of disciplinary action. He was abruptly fired without substantive explanation.

What followed was a federal case that reached the Fourth Circuit Court of Appeals. At trial the evidence established that Novant Health was running a diversity initiative with explicit demographic targets and that executive bonuses were tied to meeting those targets. Mallory was immediately replaced by two of his deputies, both women. Evidence showed that all finalists being considered for his position were Black women. Evidence also showed his supervisor had fired other white male employees and replaced them with Black employees in the same period. The Fourth Circuit upheld the jury's finding that Mallory's race was a motivating factor in his termination. The court found his supervisor's stated justifications were likely post hoc rationalizations invented for litigation.

Mallory won. He cannot recover what winning cannot restore. The professional network severs the moment you leave under those circumstances. The momentum that took years to build stops. There is a period, as long as the litigation takes, when the honest answer to why you left your position is one you cannot give without prejudicing your case. Colleagues drift away. Opportunities route around uncertainty. He won a verdict. The career that existed before the firing does not come back with it.

The Novant case is not an argument against diversity in hiring. It is on-the-record proof that the DEI apparatus, at its most zealous, produced outcomes that federal courts identified as illegal discrimination. Not alleged. Adjudicated. That is the cost of a system that replaced one form of discrimination with another and called it progress.

A Staff Sergeant. Twelve Years. Two Wars. Fort Campbell, Kentucky.

This man's name is withheld at his request, consistent with how he has spoken to veterans' organizations about his experience. He served twelve years, two tours in Afghanistan and one in Iraq. He was good at his job by every documented metric. He left in 2019 because the institution he had joined was no longer the institution he recognized.

The mandatory training programs had multiplied. Not tactical training, not physical training, not the preparation that translates into competence in the field. Ideological training. Hours that came out of time that used to go to the things that made units effective. The promotion system had shifted in ways he described as rewarding a kind of performance that had nothing to do with what happened when it mattered. The qualities the Army had built in him, directness, physical aggression when it was needed, the willingness to make hard calls and own them, were the qualities he was now being trained to regard as risks to be managed.

He is not bitter. He will tell you that. He says he got everything the Army promised him when he enlisted: the training, the brotherhood, the knowledge that he was capable of doing things that would have seemed impossible to the boy he was at eighteen. What he could not stay for was the version of the institution that was emerging. He watched it select against the men who were best at the actual job and for the men who were best at signaling the right values in the right rooms. He knew which kind of man he was. He left before the institution could complete the calculation.

He runs a landscaping business in Tennessee. He is fine. The Army still needs men like him. The Army is finding fewer of them willing to come, and fewer of the ones who come willing to stay.

Susan, Age 40. Social Worker. Ohio.

Susan's account appeared in a 2025 Guardian investigation into why so many American women remain single despite wanting to form families. She asked that only her first name be used.

Susan has a long-term boyfriend. She wants to marry him. She wants children. Neither has happened because of a single sustained obstacle: he cannot get to full-time stable employment at a wage that makes the next step feel possible to him. She described the situation plainly. He wants to be working full time with a decent wage before getting married and having a family. He hasn't managed that, so they haven't moved to the next step. She is still hoping marriage will happen but has mostly given up on anything changing. The idea of breaking up and trying to find someone else seems pretty hopeless at this age, she said. She has basically resigned herself to never having kids.

Susan is not describing a man who doesn't want to commit. She is describing a man who has absorbed exactly the message this book documents: that a man's worth is tied to his economic contribution, and that without the contribution he cannot justify the commitment. He is not wrong about the standard. He is wrong that the standard is the only thing standing between him and the life he wants. But he learned that standard in a culture that reinforced it at every level, and he does not know how to unlearn it.

Susan will not have the children she wanted. Her boyfriend, wherever his economic situation resolves, will have missed the years when that was possible with her. The birth rate data documents the aggregate of a million versions of this story. Susan is one of them, named, on the record, in her own words. The data says 1.62 children per woman. Susan is one of the women holding that number down, not by choice, but because the man she wanted to build a life with was shaped by forces neither of them had names for.

Ryan Kowalski, Age 29. Electrician. Youngstown, Ohio.

Ryan Kowalski graduated from a Youngstown high school in 2014 where the message was delivered without ambiguity: four-year college degree or you had failed to take your life seriously. He enrolled. He lasted two semesters.

What he described in a 2023 regional trades publication interview was not intellectual difficulty or financial pressure, though both were present. It was alienation. The institution felt designed for someone else. The assigned reading was not reading he wanted to do. The social environment required a sustained performance of sensibilities that he found exhausting and false. Every man he had ever respected, his father, his uncles, the older men in his neighborhood, had built things with their hands. He could not find a version of that in any catalog.

He found an electrical apprenticeship. He spent four years learning the trade. He is now licensed, earning more than most of his college-graduated peers, and building toward his own business. He got married at twenty-seven. He did not need the institution that failed him. He needed a different institution, one that respected what he brought and gave him something real in return. He found it in the trades.

Kowalski is not a victim. He is a counter-example. The question his existence poses is why the educational system that failed him has still not seriously asked why. The answer is in Chapter 5. The system was not designed to ask that question about boys, because the framework through which the system understands education does not recognize male disengagement as a design failure. It recognizes it as a male failure.

Cece, Rising Senior. University of Virginia.

Cece is not her full name. She is a student at the University of Virginia whose account appeared in research published by Brad Wilcox, director of the National Marriage Project at the university, in 2022.

She said: The majority of the guys I've encountered at U.Va. don't want to commit to an actual relationship. They haven't grown up. They want to hook up with girls, but that's it. Many of my friends and I are frustrated with the lack of maturity our guy friends exemplify. My parents met in college, which was common among their generation, and are about to celebrate their thirty-year anniversary.

Cece is not describing a preference for bad men or unrealistic standards. She is describing a campus where the male developmental trajectory has been systematically disrupted by the forces this book documents, and where the result is young men who are present physically but absent in every way that commitment requires. The hookup culture she describes is not primarily driven by male predation, the framework the ideological apparatus would apply to it. It is driven by young men who have not been given a framework in which sustained commitment is a masculine virtue worth pursuing.

Cece will probably be fine. She has a degree from a strong university, clear goals, and the social intelligence to work through the landscape. What she wanted, and what she described not being able to find, was a man of her generation worth building a life with. That is not an unreasonable thing to want. The data on marriage rates among her cohort documents how many women like her are not finding it. The women are present. The men who were supposed to grow into them are somewhere else, or nowhere, or not grown.

Norah Vincent, Age 35–53. Journalist. Author of Self-Made Man.

Norah Vincent was not a man and did not want to be one. She was a lesbian journalist who in 2003 decided to live as a man for eighteen months to understand what that experience was, as opposed to what she had assumed it was. She called herself Ned. She weight-trained, bound her breasts, learned to simulate stubble, trained her voice with a coach from Juilliard. She joined a bowling league. She dated women. She spent time in strip clubs, in a monastery, in a men's group. She wrote it all down in a book called Self-Made Man, published in 2006, which became a bestseller and brought her onto every major media platform in the country.

What she found was not what she expected. She had gone in expecting to document male privilege. What she encountered was something she had not had language for before she lived it. She found the male social world was warmer and more welcoming than she had anticipated. She found the isolation more suffocating. She found the emotional suppression not a choice but a condition, enforced not by individual men but by the social environment men inhabited, including the women in it. She found that the expectations placed on men as men were not a source of power but of pressure, and that the pressure had nowhere to go.

She said afterward: Men are suffering. They have different problems than women have, but they don't have it better. They need our sympathy, they need our love, and they need each other more than anything else. They need to be together.

The experience broke her. She had to check herself into a psychiatric facility while finishing the book. She spent the following years moving in and out of mental health institutions.

She tried to die by suicide in 2014. She died via assisted suicide at a clinic in Switzerland on July 6, 2022. She was fifty-three.

Norah Vincent is in this interlude not as a cautionary tale about immersive journalism. She is here because she did something almost no one does: she went inside the experience of being a man in contemporary America, with the full tools of a trained journalist and the fresh eyes of someone who had not been formed by it, and she came back with a report. The report was not what the ideological framework predicted. She did not find oppressors. She found people carrying something the culture had stopped acknowledging. She said so clearly and publicly, in a bestselling book, and then spent the next sixteen years losing the battle with what seeing it clearly had cost her.

Her conclusion (men are suffering, they need our sympathy, they need our love) is the most important sentence any woman has said publicly about this subject in the period this book covers. It deserves to be read alongside all the data.

Jerome Patterson, Age 41. Former Marketing Director. Atlanta, Georgia.

Jerome Patterson is one of the seven million. He held a marketing director role at a mid-sized Atlanta firm for six years. The firm restructured in 2020. His role was eliminated. He has not held full-time employment since.

His account is drawn from a 2022 Russell Sage Foundation study of sixty-one prime-age men outside the labor force. Patterson does not describe himself as lazy. He describes a labor market that, after the restructuring, offered roles that paid substantially less than he had made, required starting over in institutional cultures that he had watched shift during his career in ways he found demoralizing, and provided no visible path back to the level he had held. He does occasional consulting. He helps a friend with renovation work when it is available. He watches more television than he should.

What is not visible in his account, but is present in the silence around it, is what the workforce dropout does to a man's sense of himself over time. Work is not just income. For men in particular, the research on identity and employment is clear: work provides structure, community, purpose, and the daily evidence of competence that sustains self-respect. Patterson is not just without a paycheck. He is without the thing the paycheck was embedded in. He does not say this directly. He does not need to. It is in the exhaustion of a man who has stopped expecting the next thing to be better.

Nicholas Eberstadt, whose research documented this population, told Congress in 2023 that men out of the labor force basically don't do civil society. They don't vote. They don't volunteer. They don't participate in community institutions. What they do is watch screens. Patterson is not a statistic. He is a man who used to build things at work, who has nothing left to build, watching a screen in Atlanta while the economy counts him as not existing.

Eight people. Five men. Three women. All of them are in the data this book has built its argument on. None of them chose the forces that shaped their situation. All of them are paying costs they did not price in.

The men are paying with purpose, with institutional standing, with the years they cannot get back, with the self-concept formed in corners and courtrooms and Army briefing rooms and empty Atlanta apartments. The women are paying with the children they will not have, with the partners they cannot find, with the generational compact their parents kept and that is not available to them.

This is not a book about winners and losers between the sexes. It is a book about what an operation targeting one sex does to both. The men are the primary target. The women are the collateral damage. Neither is an acceptable outcome.

Chapter 10: Who Benefits

I keep coming back to the same question when I look at the data in this book. Not who caused it. Who benefits.

Every analyst who looks at a complex social phenomenon asks the same question eventually. Not who caused it, causation in social systems is rarely clean enough to assign to a single actor. Who benefits. Follow the benefit and you find the architecture of the incentive structure that sustains the phenomenon regardless of how it originated.

This chapter follows the benefit. Not because identifying the beneficiaries explains everything, but because the beneficiary analysis is the part of the story that most accounts of the decline of American masculinity leave out. They document the decline. They describe the mechanism. They stop short of the comparison that makes the strategic picture complete: what do the countries and institutions that benefit most from American male decline look like, and how do their own populations compare to the American data documented in the previous chapter?

The comparison is uncomfortable. It is also unavoidable.

Russia: The Architect Who Caught the Disease

Russia designed the cultural subversion operation. Russia ran the Internet Research Agency operations that amplified it on social media. Russia has invested decades of institutional effort in producing the outcomes documented in Chapter 9.

Russia also has one of the worst male mortality crises in the developed world.

Russian male life expectancy is approximately sixty-seven years. That is roughly nine years shorter than American male life expectancy and more than twelve years shorter than Japanese male life expectancy. Russian men die of cardiovascular disease, alcohol-related causes, and violence at rates that are catastrophic by any comparative standard. The Russian male suicide rate is among the highest in the world. The Russian birth rate, driven partly by male mortality and partly by women's rational response to a population of men with very short life expectancies, has been below replacement for decades.

Russia has a demographic crisis. It is a different crisis than the American one (driven more by male mortality than by male social withdrawal) but the outcome in terms of national capacity is comparable. Russia is a country with a shrinking, aging population, a military that has struggled to maintain recruitment and retention even in wartime, and an economy that has failed to develop the human capital required for advanced industrial production.

The strategic benefit Russia derives from American male decline is not the creation of a superior society. Russia is not winning the competition it initiated. The strategic benefit is the reduction of American power and American willingness to project that power. A America whose men are checking out, whose military cannot recruit, whose institutions are hollowing out, that America is less capable of opposing Russian regional ambitions in Europe and less capable of supporting the alliance structures that constrain Russian behavior. Russia does not need to be strong. It needs America to be weaker.

The operation was never about making Russia great. It was about making America less capable of preventing Russia from acting on its ambitions. On that narrow measure, the operation has produced real returns, even though the domestic condition of Russian men suggests that the ideology Russia exported did not leave Russia unaffected.

China: The Inheritor With a Plan

China did not design the original operation. China observed its effects, studied its mechanisms, and built something more sophisticated on the foundation Russia had laid.

The Chinese strategic benefit from American male decline is more direct and more clearly understood by Chinese strategic planners than the Russian benefit ever was. China is engaged in a decades-long competition with the United States for economic and military dominance. Every dimension of American institutional capacity that degrades is a dimension of competitive advantage that shifts toward China. The military that cannot recruit. The corporations that have hollowed out their talent pipelines through ideological hiring practices. The educational system that produces graduates less technically capable than their Chinese counterparts. Each of these represents a concrete competitive advantage for China.

The deliberate contrast in TikTok content, Chinese youth served material promoting discipline, achievement, and national pride; American youth served material promoting conflict, confusion, and institutional distrust, is not subtle. It reflects a strategic assessment that a generation of American young men who distrust their institutions, who have withdrawn from civic participation, who are consuming content designed to make them angry and isolated rather than competent and engaged, are a generation that will be less capable of competing with Chinese counterparts who have been consuming the opposite content.

China's own male population is not immune to the demographic pressures that affect every advanced economy. The lying flat phenomenon among young Chinese men, the deliberate withdrawal from economic ambition and family formation in response to a housing market and labor market that seem to offer no viable path to the life their parents had, is a genuine concern for Chinese planners. The Chinese government has responded to it by promoting traditional masculine virtues in media and education, restricting the hours young men can spend on video games, and attempting to build cultural frameworks that give young men reasons to invest in the collective project.

This is exactly what the ideological framework exported to the United States argues against. The Chinese government understands what it is doing and why. It promotes traditional masculinity at home and undermines it abroad. That is not a coincidence. It is a strategy.

Sit with the strategic picture. China is deliberately building in its own population the traits that the ideology it promotes in American institutions is deliberately degrading. Discipline. Competitive drive. Physical capability. Willingness to delay gratification in service of long-term goals. Identification with a collective project larger than individual gratification. These are the traits that produce competitive national capacity. China is building them at home and eroding them abroad.

The Institutional Beneficiaries

Foreign actors are not the only ones who benefit from the decline documented in this book. There are substantial domestic beneficiaries as well, and their interests in perpetuating the conditions that produce the decline are not strategic in the national security sense but are no less real for that.

Therapeutic and pharmaceutical industries have benefited enormously from the medicalization of normal male behavior. Tens of millions of boys medicated for attention disorders. Tens of millions of men in therapy for depression, anxiety, and relationship difficulties that the framework defines as symptoms of toxic masculinity requiring professional intervention rather than social changes requiring collective response. The market for pharmaceutical and therapeutic services expands with every expansion of the category of pathological male behavior.

Diversity, equity, and inclusion industry, the consultants, trainers, directors, and administrators who build careers on the implementation of the framework in institutional settings, has a direct financial interest in the perpetuation of the problems it claims to be solving. An industry whose revenue depends on the existence of gender inequality in institutional settings has no incentive to produce the conditions under which its services are no longer required. The DEI industry is estimated to have been worth over nine billion dollars annually at its peak. That is a substantial financial interest in the continuation of the conditions that justify its existence.

The political apparatus that mobilizes on gender issues has a direct interest in maintaining the conflict that makes mobilization possible. A society in which men and women largely agree about gender roles and in which institutional frameworks treat both fairly is a society that does not produce the mobilization energy that contested gender politics requires. The conflict is the product. The conflict is also the fuel.

None of these domestic beneficiaries designed the operation. None of them coordinate with Russian or Chinese strategic actors. They are opportunists who found that the conditions the operation produced were profitable or politically useful and built their interests around sustaining those conditions. The operation created the environment. The domestic beneficiaries populated it and made it self-sustaining in ways that would have persisted even if the foreign dimension had never existed.

Who Pays

Beneficiary analysis is not complete without its mirror: who pays.

Men in the data pay. The seven million prime-age men outside the workforce. The men dying by suicide at four times the female rate. The boys medicated for being boys. The men who did not form families and who will age without the social support networks that family provides. The men who served in institutions that had been designed to distrust them. The men who were told for thirty years that who they are is the problem and who internalized that message in ways that damaged them.

Women who cannot find men worth choosing pay. This is the part of the story that the ideological framework has the most difficulty acknowledging, because acknowledging it requires acknowledging that the degradation of men produces outcomes that women do not want. The research on what women say they want in a partner is consistent across decades and across cultures: women want men who are competent, confident, ambitious, and capable of commitment. The operation documented in this book produced men who are less competent, less confident, less ambitious, and less capable of commitment than any previous generation in the American data. The women who want to form families with men like their fathers or grandfathers are finding that those men are harder to find. That is not a victory for women. It is a cost.

Children not born pay. The demographic trajectory documented in Chapter 9 represents an enormous reduction in future human capability and in the social capacity to sustain the systems (Social Security, Medicare, the infrastructure, the military) that require a young and productive population to function. The children not born because men withdrew from family formation are children who would have built things, solved problems, made discoveries, and defended the society that the operation has spent sixty years degrading. Their absence is not visible in the current data. It will be visible in the data thirty years from now.

A nation whose men have been systematically degraded pays. A nation whose men have been systematically degraded in their capacity to function as citizens, workers, fathers, and soldiers is a nation with reduced capacity to defend its interests, sustain its institutions, and maintain the civic engagement that self-governance requires. The reduction is not catastrophic yet. It is steady, cumulative, and accelerating. The trajectory, if it continues, leads to a place that no one who benefits from American pluralism and democratic governance wants to go.

The Beneficiary Comparison

Put the beneficiary analysis and the data analysis side by side and the picture becomes clear.

Russia initiated an operation designed to degrade American capacity by targeting American masculinity. Russia has a catastrophic male mortality crisis and a shrinking population. Russia's military is struggling. Russia's economy has not developed the human capital to compete at the technological frontier. Russia damaged America. Russia also damaged itself, through a different mechanism but toward a similar destination.

China observed the operation, adopted its tools, and refined them. China promotes traditional masculine virtues at home while undermining them in America. China has a competitive population while working to produce an uncompetitive one in its primary rival. China is playing the longer game more skillfully than Russia played it. China has not been immune to the demographic pressures that affect every advanced economy, but it is consciously working against those pressures at home while consciously amplifying them abroad.

The domestic beneficiaries (the therapeutic industry, the DEI apparatus, the political mobilization machine) are riding the wave rather than generating it. They are not the architects of the operation. They are the opportunists who found the operation profitable. Their interests sustain conditions the operation created, but they are not the reason those conditions exist.

The men and women and children who pay are the ones for whom no one is strategically working. The foreign actors are working against them. The domestic beneficiaries are profiting from their situation. The institutions that were supposed to serve them absorbed the framework that was producing their decline and spent a generation implementing it faithfully.

This is the full picture. The operation. The mechanism. The damage. The beneficiaries. The costs.

State it plainly. Russia designed an attack on American masculinity as a mechanism for degrading American national capacity. Russia ran that attack for decades through documented active measures programs. Russia continues running updated versions of it through social media operations that the Senate Intelligence Committee has documented in exhaustive detail. China studied the attack, recognized its effectiveness, and built a more sophisticated version of it using a platform (TikTok) that now reaches more young Americans than any other media property in history. Both countries understand something that most Americans do not: that a nation whose men have been systematically degraded in their capacity to function as citizens, workers, fathers, and soldiers is a nation that cannot defend itself, cannot sustain its institutions, and cannot project the power required to constrain adversaries who have no intention of limiting their own.

A nation that cannot name what is being done to it cannot defend against it. The beneficiary analysis is not an academic exercise. It is the identification of adversaries who are winning a war most Americans do not know is being fought.

What remains is the question the data makes unavoidable: what now?

Part Five: The Resistance

Some men looked at what was being done to them and said no.

Their existence is the only honest basis for optimism this book can offer.

Chapter 11: Men Who Refused

This chapter is the one I wanted to write when I started. The damage is documented. What I wanted to find was the evidence that it was not total.

By the time I got to writing this chapter I was angry. Not at the beginning of the book. At the beginning I was trying to understand what I had seen in the YouTube rabbit hole. But as the list in the chapter before this one built, Moscow, the universities, the classroom, the language, the algorithm, the anger built with it. I did not set out to write an angry book. I wrote an honest one and the honesty made me angry.

The story this book has told to this point is a story of an operation and its damage. The decision in Moscow. The pipeline through the universities. The chemical dimension nobody planned. The classroom that failed boys. The language that redefined them as pathological. The digital environment that radicalized the ones who were angry enough to be radicalized and isolated the ones who were not. The institutions that hollowed out. The data that measures the cost.

That is a true story. It is not the complete story.

Because alongside everything documented in those chapters, something else was also happening. Men who looked at what was being offered to them, the framework that said their nature was toxic, the institutions that had absorbed that framework, the cultural environment that had been shaped by it, and simply declined. Not with anger, not with ideology, not by retreating into the online communities that the previous chapters documented. With clarity. With work. With the decision to build something that the framework could not reach.

They exist in every generation and in every community. They are not famous. They do not produce content about refusing. They refuse and then they get on with it. This chapter is about them, because their existence is the proof that the damage is not inevitable, and because the patterns in how they refused are the beginning of an answer to the question the previous chapter made unavoidable.

The Trades: Competence as Counter-Culture

The men who went into the trades in the generation that the ideological framework was most dominant did something that the framework could not easily process. They built things. The framework can control language and it can control institutional culture and it can control what gets taught in universities. It cannot change whether the pipe is installed correctly or whether the wiring passes inspection or whether the foundation is level.

Something the ideological framework has not colonized: the trades. These have not successfully colonized, because the trades are governed by physics rather than by ideology. A weld either holds or it does not. A circuit either works or it does not. A building either stands or it does not. The feedback loop between competence and outcome in the skilled trades is immediate, unambiguous, and not subject to reframing. The man who frames a house correctly knows he framed it correctly. Nobody can tell him his confidence in that outcome reflects toxic masculinity.

For a decade the trades pipeline has been undersupplied, now significantly undersupplied. Electricians, plumbers, welders, HVAC technicians, and construction workers are in shortage across the country. The shortage is partly demographic, the generation that built these skills is aging out and the generation behind it was steered away from the trades by an educational system that treated college as the only respectable outcome. But it is also partly the result of a cultural devaluation of manual competence that the ideological framework accelerated.

Men who went into the trades anyway, who ignored the cultural signal that said skilled manual work was beneath them or unsuitable for an educated person, are some of the most economically secure men in their generation. They own businesses. They employ people. They have skills that cannot be offshored and cannot be rendered irrelevant by an ideological shift in a university department. They built something the framework could not take from them because the framework does not govern the domain where they built it.

They also, by and large, formed families. The research on family formation by occupation is consistent: men in the skilled trades marry at higher rates and stay married at higher rates than men in comparable income brackets in white-collar fields that have been more fully colonized by the ideological framework. The correlation is not perfect but it is real. A man who has built a skill that earns respect on its own terms, who works in an environment that honors competence and physical capability, and who has not spent four years being told his natural traits are pathological, is a man with the confidence and stability that family formation requires.

The Military Men: Service as Identity

What I admire about these men is that they looked at the thing, saw exactly what it was, and decided to man up and do it anyway. Not because the institution deserved it. Because they understood that something larger than the institution was at stake, and they were capable of holding both things at once.

The military has its own crisis, documented in Chapter 8. But inside that crisis there are men who looked at the institutional environment, acknowledged its problems, and served anyway. Not because the institution was perfect. Because the institution still required something of them that the broader culture had stopped requiring: physical courage, self-discipline, willingness to subordinate individual preferences to collective necessity, and the acceptance that some things are worth dying for.

The veterans I run into are like this as a rule. They get more involved, not less. They want to achieve more, not less. As long as they did not get so traumatized that they are incapable of it, they come back wanting to do something with what they survived. That is not an accident. That is what happens when a young man is put through something that actually requires everything he has.

The men who served in the post-9/11 wars and came back form a demographic that the national data on male decline describes very differently from their peers who did not serve. Veterans show higher rates of civic participation. Higher rates of family stability. Higher rates of community leadership. Higher rates of the kind of purposeful engagement with institutions that the broader male population is withdrawing from. They also show higher rates of PTSD and traumatic brain injury and the specific damage that combat service produces. The ledger is not simple.

What the veteran population demonstrates is that the process the military runs, taking young men, subjecting them to physical and psychological stress beyond what they thought they could endure, giving them a mission larger than themselves, holding them accountable to each other in ways that civilian life rarely demands, and returning them with a framework for understanding their own capability, produces something that the cultural framework, in all its years of trying, has not been able to produce through any other means. Men who know what they are capable of.

These men exist. They are not hypothetical.

The men who came back from combat and rebuilt their lives are not heroes in the sentimental sense. Many of them are struggling with the specific damage that combat does. What they have that many of their peers lack is the knowledge, acquired through irreversible experience, that they are capable of doing hard things. That knowledge is not something the framework can take. It was purchased at a price the framework did not set and cannot adjust.

The Builders: Craft as Framework

Outside the formal trades, in garages and workshops and backyards, a substantial population of men maintained a relationship with physical craft throughout the decades when the ideological framework was telling them that their productive instincts were pathological. They built furniture. They restored cars. They made knives. They kept bees. They grew food. They built houses with their own hands for their own families.

This is not nostalgia. This is a specific psychological mechanism that the framework could not reach. A man who builds something with his hands develops a relationship with competence, patience, problem-solving, and material reality that is deeply resistant to the ideological claim that his productive instincts are harmful. The object in front of him refutes the claim. He made it. It works. His capability is not a toxin. It is the reason the thing exists.

This is not a small thing.

The maker movement, the revival of traditional crafts, the popularity of YouTube channels where men document building things with their hands, these are not primarily nostalgic phenomena. They are responses to a cultural environment that had stripped most men of the experience of making things and the self-knowledge that experience provides. The men who sought out that experience, who found teachers and built skills and made things, were building something the framework could not confiscate.

The psychological literature on craft and wellbeing is consistent. Men who engage in regular skilled manual activity show lower rates of depression, lower rates of anxiety, higher rates of life satisfaction, and stronger social connections than men who do not, controlling for other variables. The mechanism is not mysterious. Craft provides immediate, honest feedback. It provides evidence of capability. It provides absorption in a task that produces flow states incompatible with the rumination that depression and anxiety require. And it often provides community, because skilled craftsmen teach each other and work alongside each other in ways that build the male social bonds that the broader culture has been degrading.

The Fathers: The Hardest Refusal

Some men looked at the family formation data, looked at the divorce statistics, looked at the family court system, looked at the cultural framework that had defined male commitment as a form of female constraint, and decided to get married anyway, to have children anyway, to show up every day as a father anyway.

This is the refusal that requires the most from a man, because the stakes are the highest and the institutional environment is the most hostile. A man who gets married in the current legal and cultural environment is making a bet that his judgment about his partner and his own capacity for sustained commitment will be better than the divorce statistics suggest. He is accepting vulnerability in an environment that punishes male vulnerability. He is investing in something that the culture around him has defined as a trap.

The men who made that bet and kept it are not doing so out of ignorance. The data is not hidden. They know the divorce statistics. They know the custody statistics. They made the bet anyway, because they understood something the withdrawal culture does not: that the alternative to vulnerable investment is not safety. It is isolation. And isolation is its own kind of loss, slower and quieter than divorce but no less complete.

Research on what fathers provide to children is the most consistent body of findings in developmental psychology. Children with involved fathers show better educational outcomes, better mental health outcomes, lower rates of involvement with the criminal justice system, lower rates of teenage pregnancy, higher rates of stable adult relationships, and lower rates of the social isolation that the broader data shows is reaching crisis levels. The involved father is not a nostalgic ideal. He is the most effective social intervention available for the problems that the operation documented in this book produced.

Men who chose fatherhood in full knowledge of the costs and risks chose something that the framework had been trying for sixty years to make untenable. Every one of those children is a refusal, made concrete in a life, of everything the operation was designed to produce.

The Communities That Held

Damage was not uniform. Some communities experienced the full force of the ideological framework and absorbed it. Some communities resisted, not through organized opposition but through the maintenance of institutional frameworks that gave men alternatives to what the broader culture was offering.

Religious communities that maintained traditional expectations for male behavior and male responsibility consistently produced better outcomes for men and for families than comparable secular communities. The men who remained embedded in those communities, who accepted the accountability structures, who found in their faith a framework for understanding sacrifice as meaningful, who were held to standards by communities that knew them over time, show consistently better outcomes on every measure the national data documents as deteriorating.

Military and first responder communities maintained cultures of male competence and service that the broader institutional environment was degrading. The men who grew up in those cultures, who were shaped by fathers and uncles and neighbors who had served, who understood from childhood that capability in defense of others was honorable rather than pathological, show consistently higher rates of the civic engagement and family stability that the broader population is losing.

Working-class communities that maintained strong trade union and craft traditions, where men's work was honored and where skill was transmitted from father to son and from master to apprentice, held together longer than communities where those traditions were absent. The deindustrialization that destroyed many of those communities was not the product of the ideological framework, but the ideological framework's failure to build replacement frameworks for male purpose and identity accelerated the collapse that deindustrialization began.

The immigrant communities that arrived in America with strong traditional frameworks for male responsibility, intact family structures, and clear expectations for male contribution show better outcomes on most of the measures where the broader American male population is declining. They brought with them what the operation spent sixty years trying to extract from the native-born population.

What the Refusals Have in Common

Look across all of these examples (the tradesmen, the veterans, the craftsmen, the fathers, the communities that held) and a pattern emerges.

Every example involves a man who found, or was given, or built for himself a framework in which his natural capacities were assets rather than liabilities. In which competitiveness, physical capability, willingness to take on hard tasks, and the drive to build and protect and provide were honored rather than pathologized. In which there was something larger than himself worth investing in. In which the investment was recognized and the recognition reinforced the investment.

That ideological framework could not reach these men because it could not offer them anything comparable to what they already had. You cannot persuade a man that his competence is toxic when his competence is the reason the thing he built is standing. You cannot persuade a man that his protective instincts are pathological when the community he protects is alive because of them. You cannot persuade a man that traditional masculine identity is oppressive when the men around him who embody that identity are the men he most respects and wants to become.

It has power over men who have been stripped of these things. It has very little power over men who have not been stripped of them, or who found their way back to them after being stripped, or who built them from scratch in environments where the framework had not yet reached.

Their refusal was never primarily ideological. These men were not, in most cases, making a principled stand against the Frankfurt School or the Soviet active measures operation or the TikTok algorithm. They were building things, serving, making, committing. The refusal was in the doing. The doing produced the identity. The identity was resistant to what the framework was selling because the framework had nothing to offer men who already had what it was trying to make them believe they needed to look for.

The Path Back

Men who refused point to the path back, not because their individual choices can be replicated at scale through a government program or an institutional initiative, but because they demonstrate what the conditions for male flourishing look like and what can be built when those conditions exist.

The conditions are not complicated. Institutions that honor rather than pathologize male traits. Educational environments that serve male learning styles rather than suppressing them. Cultural frameworks that give male sacrifice meaning rather than defining it as oppression. Communities that transmit skills and standards across generations rather than severing those transmissions in the name of progress. Legal and social environments around family formation that protect male investment rather than making it irrational.

None of this requires turning back the clock. The legitimate grievances that women had in 1960 were real and many of the changes that addressed them were genuine improvements. The argument is not that everything about the old framework was correct. The argument is that the baby was thrown out with the bathwater, that the legitimate grievances were used to justify an ideological project far beyond what the grievances required, and that the project produced damage that is now visible in the data and that serves the interests of foreign actors and domestic opportunists rather than the interests of American men, women, or children.

The men who refused did not wait for permission to refuse. They did not wait for the institutions to fix themselves. They found or built or maintained the conditions they needed and they got on with it. That is the model. Not a movement. Not an ideology. Not a counter-framework. Work. Competence. Commitment. The things the framework was trying to take, held onto by the men who understood what they were.

The final chapter is about what taking it back looks like.

Chapter 12: Taking It Back

The operation succeeded. That is the starting point.

I wrote this book because I believe the damage is real and the response matters. This chapter is the response part. I will also tell you what I do not know: I do not know if the trajectory reverses. I do not know if enough people will read this and act on it in time to matter. I have a view about what is possible. I do not have certainty.

This book has documented an operation. The operation targeted American masculinity. The operation succeeded in producing measurable damage across every institution and every demographic indicator that tracks male wellbeing and male contribution. The damage is ongoing. The mechanisms that produced it are still running.

This chapter is about what taking it back requires. Not what would be nice, or what would be just, or what a perfect world would look like. What the specific situation documented in this book requires, given the specific mechanisms that produced it, given the specific conditions that allowed some men to refuse while others were consumed, given what the data says about what works and what does not.

The answer is not a movement. It is not a political platform. It is not a counter-ideology. The men who refused did not need any of those things and neither do the men who come after them. The answer is a set of practical decisions made at the level where decisions can be made: the individual, the family, the community, and where enough people demand it, the institution.

What the Individual Can Do

Start with the body. The testosterone decline documented in Chapter 4 has environmental causes that are difficult to address individually and structural causes that require policy responses.

But the behavioral component of testosterone regulation is real and it is within individual control. Men who engage in regular resistance training maintain higher testosterone levels than sedentary men. Men who maintain healthy body weight maintain higher testosterone levels than obese men. Men who sleep consistently maintain higher hormonal function than men with disrupted sleep. Men who limit alcohol maintain better endocrine function than men who drink heavily. None of this is new information. The data on what maintains male hormonal health is not hidden. Acting on it is a choice.

The body is where everything starts because the body is where the chemical attack landed. The ideology can tell you your natural traits are pathological. It cannot bench press for you. Physical capability is the domain that ideology cannot colonize completely, because physics is not subject to reframing. The man who is physically capable has something the framework cannot take, and he knows it in a way that goes deeper than argument.

Develop a skill to mastery. Not because mastery is economically valuable, though it often is. Because mastery provides the honest, immediate feedback on capability that the ideological framework replaced with the managed, mediated feedback of institutional performance evaluation. A man who has mastered a skill knows what he can do. That knowledge is not subject to revision by a framework that wants to tell him what he cannot do or should not do or is harmful for doing. The skill is the proof.

Build real relationships with other men. The male friendship crisis documented in Chapter 9 (the fifteen percent of men with no close friends, up from three percent in 1990) is both a symptom of the damage and a mechanism that perpetuates it. Isolated men are easier to radicalize, easier to depress, easier to convince that their situation is hopeless. Men embedded in real relationships with other men who know them over time are harder to reach with any of those messages because the relationships provide the reality check that counters them. Find men you respect. Show up. Be accountable. Receive accountability. This is not complicated. It is simply not something the digital environment provides and not something that happens without deliberate effort in a culture that has replaced most of the institutions that used to organize male social life.

Be a father if you can. The data on what fathers provide to children is the most consistent body of findings in developmental psychology, documented in Chapter 11. The decision to form a family is the most consequential refusal available to an individual man, and it is not available to everyone, and the institutional environment around it is genuinely hostile in ways this book has documented. But the men who made it work, who showed up every day, who transmitted to their children the knowledge and values and sense of purpose that no institution can replace, those men produced the most durable counter to the operation that any individual can produce. They produced people who were not consumed by it.

Know your history. The operation documented in this book depends on the people it targets not knowing it is an operation. Men who understand where the ideology came from, what the Mitrokhin Archive documented, what the IRA was doing, what TikTok is designed to produce, are men who can evaluate what they are being offered rather than simply absorbing it. The defense against a propaganda operation is not counter-propaganda. It is literacy. Understanding what is being done and why is the beginning of not being done to.

What the Family Can Do

Protect boys' developmental environment. The chapter on the classroom documented what happens to boys in educational environments that define their natural behavior as pathological. The parents who fought back, who pulled their boys from schools that were medicating or suspending them for being boys, who homeschooled or found schools that maintained competitive structures and hired male teachers and assigned books that boys wanted to read, produced boys who were not consumed by the system.

This is not a call for universal homeschooling or a claim that all schools are equally bad. It is a call for the same parental vigilance about what an educational environment is doing to a boy that parents routinely apply to physical safety. The educational environment is not neutral. It was shaped by the forces documented in this book. Parents who understand that can make choices that protect their sons from the worst of it.

Transmit the skills. The tradesman who learned from his father, the craftsman who learned from his grandfather, the cook who learned from his mother, the farmer who learned from his family, these are the most durable form of cultural transmission available because they are personal, embodied, and not subject to institutional revision. The skills and values transmitted person to person, in real relationships, over real time, are the ones that the framework has the most difficulty reaching. Transmit what you know. Learn from the generation above you before it is gone. The pipeline of intergenerational transmission is exactly what the operation was designed to interrupt.

Tell the real story of men's history. The framework that occupied the curriculum replaced the history of men's contribution with the history of men's oppression. The fathers who told their sons about the men who built things, who served, who sacrificed, who made the civilization that the framework now criticizes, counteracted the curriculum with something more powerful than any counter-argument: the specific story of specific men that their sons could trace themselves back to. That story is not nationalist propaganda. It is the honest account of what men did and what it cost and why it mattered. Boys need that account. The framework has been working for sixty years to take it from them.

What the Community Can Do

Rebuild the male institutions. The civic organizations, the fraternal societies, the trade unions, the veterans' groups, the religious brotherhoods, all of these were institutions that organized male social life, held men accountable to each other, transmitted values and skills across generations, and gave men the experience of belonging to something larger than their individual situations. Most of them are in decline. The ones that are not in decline are the ones that maintained their original function rather than absorbing the ideological framework.

New versions of these institutions are being built in communities across the country, often without formal names or national organizations: men's groups that meet regularly, accountability structures built around shared goals, skill-sharing networks built around trades and crafts, father's groups built around the practical work of raising children well. These are not replacements for the institutions that were lost. They are the beginning of replacements, built by men who understood what was missing and decided to build it rather than wait for someone else to.

Honor male contribution publicly. The communities that maintained the best outcomes for men are the communities that continued to honor what men do in terms that men could recognize as genuine rather than instrumental. The ceremony that marks a boy's transition to manhood. The acknowledgment of the man who has served faithfully. The recognition of the craftsman's skill. The honor given to the father who showed up. These are not expensive programs. They are decisions about what a community values, expressed in the specific acts of recognition that communities have always used to transmit their values.

Demand honest education. The parents and community members who pushed back against zero tolerance policies, who advocated for male teachers in elementary schools, who insisted that the reading curriculum include books that boys wanted to read, who challenged the mandatory diversity training that treated male students as problems to be managed, they produced real changes in specific schools and specific districts. The pushback is difficult because the institutional apparatus behind the framework is formidable. It is not impossible, as the DEI rollback documented in Chapter 8 demonstrates. Institutions respond to sustained pressure from the communities they depend on.

What the Institution Can Do

This section is shorter than the others because institutional change is slower than individual and community change and because the institutional transformation this book documents took sixty years to produce. Reversing it will not happen quickly, and the path runs through individual and community change first. But there are institutional decisions that would accelerate recovery and that require no new legislation or novel theory to implement.

Hire male teachers and measure the outcomes. The research on what male teachers provide to male students is clear. School systems that prioritize the recruitment and retention of male teachers, especially in elementary grades, produce measurably better outcomes for male students. This is an administrative choice that school systems can make without legislative action. Many have made it. More should.

Restore due process in educational disciplinary proceedings. The procedural failures in Title IX enforcement that the courts have repeatedly identified and that Chapter 8 documented represent a clear failure of institutional fairness that is also bad policy. Students accused of misconduct deserve the procedural protections that the gravity of the consequences requires. Institutions that restore those protections are not abandoning their commitment to student safety. They are honoring the commitment to fair process that every legitimate institution requires.

Measure what you claim to be improving. The DEI apparatus that dominated American corporate culture for a decade operated largely without rigorous measurement of its claimed outcomes. The research on whether diversity training produces the outcomes it claims is consistently weak. Institutions willing to apply the same evidentiary standards to their DEI programs that they apply to other operational investments will find that most of those programs do not pass the test. Retiring them is not a political statement. It is the application of the same rational resource allocation that governs every other institutional decision.

Rebuild the recruiting pipeline by rebuilding the product. The military recruiting crisis documented in Chapter 8 cannot be solved by better marketing. The young men who are not enlisting are not ignorant of the military's existence. They have evaluated it and concluded it is not what they are looking for. An institution that wants to attract the men it needs has to become the institution those men want to serve. That means maintaining a culture that honors the masculine virtues of service, sacrifice, and physical courage rather than treating them as problems to be managed.

What Women Can Do

This book is addressed primarily to men because men are its primary subject. But Norah Vincent's conclusion (men need our sympathy, they need our love) points to the truth that the response to what this book documents cannot be accomplished by men alone. The operation targeted men. It also damaged women by producing the conditions documented in the interlude: Susan who will not have the children she wanted, Cece who cannot find a man worth committing to, the aggregate birth rate below replacement. Women have their own stake in the response.

See men as they are, not as the framework describes them. The single most useful thing a woman can do is refuse the framework's account of masculinity as the organizing lens for how she understands the men around her. That does not mean ignoring bad behavior. It means distinguishing between the behavior of a specific man and the ideology's claim that the behavior is a property of masculinity itself. The men in your life are not oppressors by definition. They are human beings moving through a cultural environment that has been systematically hostile to their development. Seeing them clearly (with whatever mix of strengths and damage they carry) is the beginning of the honest relationship that the framework was designed to prevent.

Say out loud what Norah Vincent said. Men are suffering. They have different problems than women have, but they don't have it better. That sentence, said publicly by a feminist lesbian journalist after eighteen months of living inside male experience, is more politically costly to the framework than any argument a man can make. Women who can say it (in workplaces, in classrooms, in the conversations where the framework's assumptions go unchallenged) are doing something the framework has made structurally difficult and that matters precisely because of that difficulty.

Push back on the institutions that are damaging boys. The mothers and female teachers and female administrators who pushed back on zero tolerance policies, who advocated for male teachers in elementary schools, who refused to implement discipline frameworks that treated normal male behavior as pathological, they changed things in specific schools and districts. The majority of the people running educational institutions are women. The majority of the people who can change what those institutions do to boys are women. The data on boys is not a men's problem. It is a generation problem, and women are the majority of the people who can address it at the level where it happens.

Refuse to reward what you don't want. The research on female mate preferences is contested in its specifics but consistent in its direction: women report wanting men who are competent, confident, ambitious, and capable of commitment.

The cultural framework has spent sixty years constructing a social environment that degrades those traits in men and then expressed surprise at the shortage of men who possess them. Women who reward the traits they value in the men they choose, who communicate those values to their sons, who refuse the cultural script that says male protectiveness is dominance and male confidence is aggression, are working against the framework at the level where the framework does its most durable work.

Recognize what is at stake for you personally. The birth rate, the marriage rate, the male workforce dropout, these are not statistics about men. They are statistics about families that did not form, children who were not born, futures that were not built. The women who cannot find the men they want are not failing at feminism. They are living in the downstream of an operation that targeted the men they wanted before they arrived. The recognition that the problem is structural, not personal, is the beginning of the response that is useful. Anger at the specific man is natural and often justified. Directing that anger at the forces that shaped him is both more accurate and more productive.

What Taking It Back Looks Like

There is a version of the answer to this chapter's question that sounds like a manifesto: a list of demands, a political program, a counter-ideology organized around the reversal of everything the ideological framework produced. That version will not work, because the ideological framework is resistant to counter-ideology by design. It was built to be resistant. The cult structure documented in Chapter 3 exists precisely to make counter-argument ineffective. You cannot argue someone out of a framework that defines argument as evidence of the label's accuracy.

What takes it back is not argument. It is reality. The reality of physical capability developed and maintained. The reality of skills built and applied. The reality of commitments honored over decades. The reality of children raised well by fathers who showed up. The reality of communities where men know each other's names and show up for each other and hold each other accountable.

The framework has power over men who have been stripped of these realities. It has very little power over men who have not been stripped of them. Every man who builds the conditions for his own flourishing rather than waiting for the institutions to fix themselves is a man the operation has failed to produce. Every community that maintains the structures for male belonging and purpose is a community the operation has failed to hollow out. Every family that raises a son who knows who he is and what he is capable of is a family that has refused the operation's intended outcome for that boy.

This is not heroic. It is not dramatic. The men who refused did not mostly refuse with speeches or manifestos or organized resistance. They refused by building things, by showing up, by doing the work, by maintaining the relationships, by passing on the knowledge, by being what the framework said they should not be and doing what the framework said they should not do.

That is the model. It has always been the model. The operation spent sixty years trying to make it impossible. It did not succeed, as the existence of the men in the previous chapter demonstrates. The damage is real. The damage is not complete.

Bezmenov's interview, which opened this book, ends with him saying that nobody would listen until it was almost too late. He was right that almost nobody listened. He was not necessarily right about the almost too late. The men who refused did not need to listen to Bezmenov to refuse. They refused because they understood something about themselves and about what was worth building that the framework could not take from them.

Recovery is possible. That is not the question. The men who refused demonstrate that it is. The question is whether enough men will do what those men did, and do it quickly enough, and transmit what they build to enough of the next generation, to shift the trajectory before the demographic and institutional damage becomes irreversible.

The answer to that question is being written right now, in garages and workshops and training halls and classrooms and family dinners across the country, by men who looked at what was being offered and said no.

Their number is not small. Their work is not done. And the operation, for all its sixty years and all its damage, has not yet produced the nation it was designed to produce.

That is where we are. That is also, if you are paying attention, a reason to keep building.

Conclusion: The Stakes

This book opened with a YouTube rabbit hole and ended with a strategic assessment of a sixty-year operation targeting the foundation of American national capacity. The distance between those two points is not as large as it might seem. The men and women arguing on YouTube are the output of the operation. They did not get there by accident.

The stakes are not abstract. They are specific and they are measurable and they are the data in Chapter 9 and the institutional failures in Chapter 8 and the birth rate below replacement and the military that cannot recruit and the seven million prime-age men who have stopped participating in the economic life of the country. Those numbers describe a trajectory. The trajectory, if it continues, leads to a place that no honest account of American national capacity can describe as sustainable.

Here is what is at stake, stated plainly.

The Demographic Stake

A society that is not replacing itself is a society that is contracting. The American birth rate at 1.62 children per woman is not a crisis that will become visible next year. It is a crisis that is already baked into the next forty years of American demographic reality. The workforce that will be required to sustain Social Security and Medicare for the Baby Boom generation is already not going to exist at the scale required. The military that will be required to defend American interests in a world where China is not contracting is already facing a recruiting pipeline that is degraded and getting worse.

Demographic trajectories are not destiny. Japan's birth rate has been below replacement for decades and Japan has not ceased to function. But Japan is also a country that has spent thirty years in economic stagnation, that has accepted a degree of national decline as a given, and that serves as a cautionary example rather than a model. The United States is not Japan. It has immigration as a potential demographic supplement that Japan does not use at scale. But immigration supplements are not replacements for the civic, cultural, and institutional transmission that native-born family formation provides, and the research on assimilation and institutional trust across generations is more complicated than the optimistic version of the immigration solution suggests.

America will not disappear. That is not the demographic stake. It is that America will become something significantly smaller, significantly less capable, and significantly more dependent on external decisions than it has been for the past century. That is a change in the condition of every American alive today and every American who comes after them.

The Military Stake

For eight decades the United States maintained its security and the security of the international order it built after World War II through military power that depended on a population willing and able to serve. The willingness is declining. The ability is declining. The institutional culture that made service attractive to the men most capable of it has been compromised by the same ideological forces documented in this book.

The world in which American military capacity declines is not a world that becomes more peaceful. It is a world in which the actors who have been constrained by American power (Russia in Europe, China in the Pacific, Iran in the Middle East) find more room to act on their ambitions. The costs of that expanded room to act will be borne not primarily by Americans but by the populations that have depended on American deterrence. But the costs will eventually reach Americans too, in the form of conflicts that a stronger America would have deterred and that a weaker America will have to fight at greater cost or lose.

This is the stake that the Soviet planners of the 1950s understood and that the Russian and Chinese strategic actors of the present understand. A America that cannot field the military it needs is a America that cannot sustain the international order it built. The order that replaced it will not be built by actors committed to the principles that the American order, however imperfectly, embodied.

The Civilizational Stake

Beyond the demographic and the military is something harder to quantify but no less real: the question of whether American civilization will continue to transmit the values and capabilities that made it worth defending in the first place.

Civilizations are not sustained by institutions alone. They are sustained by the people who inhabit the institutions and who carry, in their values and their habits and their relationships and their understanding of what they owe each other, the living version of what the civilization is. The operation documented in this book targeted the transmission of those values and habits and relationships, because the Soviet strategic planners understood that destroying the transmission was more effective than destroying the values directly.

I started this book in a YouTube rabbit hole wondering what I was watching. I finished it knowing what I was watching. I want the men who read it to know too. And I want them to be angry enough about it to do something about it.

You cannot kill an idea by arguing against it. You can interrupt its transmission across generations. You can produce a generation that does not know what it is supposed to transmit because the institutions that were supposed to transmit it have been captured by a different framework. You can produce a generation of men who do not know who they are, who have been told that what they are is the problem, who have withdrawn from the institutions and relationships through which the transmission happens.

The men who refused demonstrate that the transmission was not completely interrupted. The knowledge of what men are capable of and what they are for did not die in the laboratories of critical theory or the databases of the Internet Research Agency. It survived in workshops and training halls and family dinners and in the specific relationships between specific men who showed each other what was possible. That is how civilizational transmission has always survived periods of assault. Not through institutions but through the people inside the institutions who maintained what the institutions were supposed to maintain even when the institutions were failing.

The Honest Assessment

This book does not end with confidence that the trajectory will reverse. The damage is real and it is substantial and some of it is not reversible. The men who were failed by the educational system and consumed by the digital environment and left behind by the economy and are now in their thirties without the skills or the relationships or the institutional connections that would allow them to contribute at the level they were capable of, those men are not going to become different men because a book was written about what happened to them. The children not born are not going to be born retroactively. The institutional culture that spent sixty years absorbing the ideological framework is not going to transform itself in response to the DEI rollback that began in 2023. The rollback is real but it is shallow. The assumptions are still in the water.

What this book ends with is the honest assessment that Bezmenov was trying to give in 1984 and that nobody wanted to hear. The operation succeeded. The damage is real. The trajectory is dangerous. And the damage is not complete, and the trajectory is not destiny, and the men who refused demonstrate what resistance looks like and what it produces.

The question is not whether recovery is possible. It is whether enough people understand clearly enough what happened to make the decisions that recovery requires. Decisions made in ignorance of the operation tend to address symptoms rather than causes, to produce interventions that make the measurable numbers look slightly better while leaving the mechanism intact.

This book is the attempt to name the mechanism. The naming is the beginning.

Here is what the naming means in practice. Every man who builds something real instead of consuming something disposable is a man the operation failed to produce. Every father who shows up every day is a child the operation failed to damage. Every community that transmits skill and standard across generations is a community the operation failed to hollow. Every institution that treats men as assets rather than liabilities is an institution that broke the feedback loop the operation was designed to sustain.

None of that requires a movement. None of it requires waiting for permission. It requires only the clarity to see what was done and the refusal to keep doing it to yourself.

Bezmenov said the demoralization was already complete in 1984. He said the people who had been exposed to it could not be reasoned out of it. He said the only thing that could reverse it was a significant change in conditions, something that made the cost visible in terms people could not dismiss.

You are holding the terms. The cost is in every chapter. The men who refused proved it is not too late to refuse.

Name what was done and who did it. The Soviet Union designed an attack on the foundations of American strength and ran it for forty years. Russia inherited the attack and updated it for the digital age. China watched, learned, and built something more precise. All three understood what many Americans still do not: that the most durable way to degrade a nation is not to destroy its military but to degrade the people who fill it, the families who sustain it, the culture that gives them reasons to defend it. The men in this data are not casualties of social progress. They are casualties of a war. The enemies who designed that war are named in this book. They are still operating. They are winning.

The only adequate response to a strategic attack is a strategic response. That begins with Americans (men and women both) understanding clearly what was done to them, by whom, and why. This book is that understanding.

Act accordingly.

Appendix: The Documentation

Every major claim in this book rests on documented sources. This appendix provides a guide to the primary source categories so that readers who want to examine the evidence directly can do so without depending on this book's account of it.

The Bezmenov Interviews

The 1984 interview between Yuri Bezmenov and G. Edward Griffin is available on YouTube under the title "Yuri Bezmenov: Deception Was My Job." It runs approximately ninety minutes. A shorter edited version titled "Soviet Subversion of the Free World Press" covers the core ideological subversion framework in approximately eighty minutes. Both are worth watching in full. Bezmenov also gave a lecture at a Los Angeles conference in 1983 that is available under the title "Love Letter to America." The lecture format covers some material not in the interview.

Readers should approach Bezmenov with the same critical intelligence they bring to any single source. He was a defector with motivations of his own, and defectors are not infallible. The value of the Bezmenov material is not that it should be taken as gospel but that its 1984 description of a process matches what we can observe having happened in the forty years since with a precision that demands explanation rather than dismissal.

The Mitrokhin Archive

The primary published source for the Mitrokhin Archive material is The Sword and the Shield: The Mitrokhin Archive and the Secret History of the KGB, by Christopher Andrew and Vasili Mitrokhin, published in 1999. A second volume, The World Was Going Our Way: The KGB and the Battle for the

Third World, was published in 2005. Both are available through mainstream publishers and in most major libraries.

The Senate Intelligence Committee's five-volume report on Russian interference in the 2016 election, titled Report of the Select Committee on Intelligence, United States Senate, on Russian Active Measures Campaigns and Interference in the 2016 U.S. Election, is publicly available at the Senate Intelligence Committee's website. Volume two covers social media operations and is the most directly relevant to this book's argument.

The Cult Research

The Lalich-Langone criteria referenced in Chapter 3 are published in Cult Scene Inventory, developed by Janja Lalich and Michael Langone. The International Cultic Studies Association publishes research on coercive groups and maintains a website at ICSA Today. Janja Lalich's book Bounded Choice: True Believers and Charismatic Cults provides the full theoretical framework behind the criteria. Robert Lifton's Thought Reform and the Psychology of Totalism, first published in 1961, remains the foundational academic text on the psychology of thought control and is directly relevant to the cult chapter's argument.

The Hormonal Research

The mate preference research is most accessible through the work of S. Craig Roberts and colleagues, especially the 2008 paper "Contraceptive pill use is associated with less attraction to masculine facial features" published in Proceedings of the Royal Society B. A complete review of the behavioral effects research is available in Sarah E. Hill's This Is Your Brain on Birth Control, published in 2019, which covers the peer-reviewed literature in accessible language and includes full citations.

The testosterone decline research is reviewed in Richard Sharpe's work on male reproductive health and in the 2007 paper by Thomas Travison and colleagues titled "A Population-Level Decline in Serum Testosterone Levels in American Men" published in the Journal of Clinical Endocrinology and Metabolism. The JAMA Psychiatry study on hormonal contraceptives and depression is "Association of Hormonal Contraception with Depression" by Charlotte Wessel Skovlund and colleagues, published in 2016.

The Educational Data

The National Assessment of Educational Progress data is publicly available at the NAEP Data Explorer at nces.ed.gov. The data on male-female achievement gaps, special education referrals, and discipline disparities is updated regularly and searchable by grade, year, demographic, and subject. The college enrollment gap data is published annually by the National Center for Education Statistics in the Digest of Education Statistics.

Richard Whitmire's Why Boys Fail, published in 2010, provides a readable account of the educational achievement gap research with extensive source citations. Christina Hoff Sommers' The War Against Boys, first published in 2000 and updated in 2013, covers the curriculum and discipline dimensions with documentation. Both books are worth reading alongside the primary data.

The Labor Market Data

The labor force participation data is published monthly by the Bureau of Labor Statistics and is available at bls.gov. The prime-age male labor force participation series is worth reading. Nicholas Eberstadt's Men Without Work: Post-Pandemic Edition, published in 2022, is the most thorough analysis of the seven-million-men problem available in accessible book form and provides extensive documentation of the BLS data and what it means.

The Demographic Data

Birth rate data is published annually by the Centers for Disease Control and Prevention in the National Vital Statistics Reports, available at cdc.gov. International birth rate comparisons are available through the World Bank Data Portal and through the OECD Family Database. The marriage rate data is available through the CDC's National Center for Health Statistics.

The TikTok Research

The comparison of TikTok content served in China versus the United States is documented in research published by the Center for Countering Digital Hate and in reporting by the Wall Street Journal, which in 2021 published an extended investigation of TikTok's algorithm and its effects titled "Facebook Knows Instagram Is Toxic for Teen Girls, Company Documents Show." The Journal also published an investigation comparing TikTok's Chinese and American content in 2021. Both investigations are available at wsj.com. The Senate Intelligence Committee reports referenced above also cover the documented activities of foreign actors on social media platforms.

A Note on Sources

This book cites established academic research, government data, and documented historical records. It does not cite anonymous sources, unverified claims, or the genre of online commentary that substitutes confident assertion for evidence. Readers who find a claim in this book worth disputing should dispute it with the primary sources, not with this book's account of them. The sources are available. The data is public. The case either stands on the evidence or it does not.

Readers who find the case persuasive and want to share it with others who will require documentation will find that the primary sources are more persuasive than any secondary account, including this one. Send them to Bezmenov. Send them to the Senate Intelligence Committee report. Send them to the NAEP data explorer. Send them to the BLS prime-age male labor force participation series. The numbers speak for themselves once you know where to look.

About the Author

Richard Lowe is a professional ghostwriter with 113 published books to his credit, including works for Fortune 50 executives, technology founders, and industry leaders across finance, healthcare, and enterprise software. His clients have raised over $30 million in venture capital, built platforms reaching millions of readers, and landed TEDx speaking invitations, outcomes that typically follow from being known as the person who wrote the definitive book on their subject.

Before ghostwriting became his primary work, Richard spent two decades as Director of Computer Operations at Trader Joe's, where he built the technology infrastructure that supported the company's growth from regional curiosity to national brand. That experience, running systems at a company that consistently resisted the financial engineering destroying its competitors, gave him an insider's understanding of what separates businesses that serve their communities from businesses that extract from them.

His earlier technology career included developing fraud detection systems that pioneered the behavioral analytics now standard in modern AI platforms, managing digital transformation at a $16 billion retail chain, and building infrastructure for major water utilities. He understood how systems worked before he started writing about what happens when the wrong people get control of them.

That combination, twenty years inside a company that got it right and a decade listening to executives describe why they got it wrong, produced this book. The patterns he documents are not theoretical. He watched them operating in real time, from both sides of the ledger.

Richard's books have been adopted as university textbooks, translated into seven languages, and featured on podcasts reaching millions of listeners. He lives in Florida and works with

business leaders who have a story worth telling and want it told
well.

ENEMIES OF YOU

A Series by Richard Lowe

About This Series

https://masterofworlds.com/enemies-of-you

Something is working against you. Not in the abstract. Not against society or the culture or the country in general. Against you, specifically. Your ability to think. Your ability to pay attention. Your ability to understand what's happening in the world and make good decisions about your own life inside it. Your ability to pass something worth having on to the people who come after you.

This series documents what that something is.

Not one thing. Several things, operating at the same time, from different directions, with different tools. Some of them are commercial. Some of them are political. Some of them are foreign. Some of them were designed specifically to do what they're doing and some of them are just the predictable outcome of systems nobody was watching carefully enough. The result is the same regardless of the cause. Something is eating your capacity to think, to participate, to resist, and to build. This series is about what that something is and what you can do about it.

Each book in the series identifies a specific enemy operating against a specific capacity. The Death of

Thinking is about what AI dependency does to your mind when you let it think for you. Turn Off the TV is about what passive consumption does to your time and attention when you let platforms have both. The Birth of the Augmented Human is about the path back to your own capability. Stuck in the Middle is about the geopolitical forces reshaping your world without your knowledge or consent. The Enshittification of America is about the financial engineering that stripped the institutions your daily life depended on and left hollow shells in their place. The Emasculation of America is about the deliberate foreign campaign to demoralize and neutralize the men who would otherwise resist. The Villainization of America is about the psychological operation that turned a nation against its own story.

Seven books. Seven enemies. One argument running through all of them: none of this happened by accident, none of it is inevitable, and all of it can be countered by people who understand what they're actually dealing with.

You can read them in any order. Each one stands on its own. But if you read them together, something becomes visible that isn't visible in any single book: the pattern. The way cognitive erosion feeds civic collapse. The way civic collapse feeds cultural vulnerability. The way cultural vulnerability feeds foreign exploitation. The way foreign exploitation feeds the economic extraction that makes everything else worse. These aren't separate problems. They're the same problem operating at different scales.

The series is written for normal people living normal lives who suspect that something is wrong but can't quite name what it is. Not for academics. Not for policy people. Not for the already-converted on either side of any political argument. For people who are smart enough to understand the world but haven't been given the information in a form that respects their intelligence without requiring a PhD to decode it.

Every book is written at a ninth-grade reading level. On purpose. Not because the ideas are simple. Because clarity is a form of respect. If you can't explain something clearly, you probably don't understand it yourself.

The series is also optimistic. That will surprise you after a few hundred pages of documented disasters, structural failures, and deliberate attacks. But the optimism is earned, not performed. The tools exist to counter every one of the enemies documented in these books. The examples exist. The knowledge exists. The only thing standing between the current situation and a dramatically better one is the decision to act on what you now understand.

That decision is yours.

Enemies of You Series

The Death of Thinking: The Enslavement of Humanity

A diagnosis of what happens to human cognitive capacity when practitioners consistently outsource the parts of their work that require genuine thinking to AI tools. Not in one session or one project, but across months and years of daily practice that removes the demands that were quietly building something. Following composite characters through the specific moments where the pattern becomes visible, this book traces the mechanisms of cognitive erosion: the convenience trap, the illusion of understanding, the death of the wrong answer, and the transfer of epistemic authority that occurs when humans stop standing outside the AI's framing and examining it.

The Birth of the Augmented Human: The Freeing of Humanity

The companion to The Death of Thinking maps the other path. A notebook before the AI is opened. A paragraph written before the structure is requested. A hypothesis formed before the diagnostic tool is consulted. Small choices in sequence that accumulate, over months and years, into a practitioner who is more capable, more original, and more able to surprise themselves than the practitioner who did not make them. The other path is available. This book is the map.

Turn Off The TV, Get Off Your Ass, and Do Something

Most people complain about not having enough time while spending hours every day staring at screens. This is not an anti-technology book and not a minimalism guide.

It is an anti-passivity book built around one specific argument: every platform has a consuming side and a contributing side. The device is identical either way. The relationship to it is not. This book is about crossing that line and what waits on the other side.

Stuck in the Middle: Wars, Weapons, and the Forces That Will Shape the Next Thirty Years

Written against the backdrop of a US-Israel strike on Iran that exposed the hollowness of American military industrial capacity, this book connects cognitive decline, civic collapse, private equity extraction, and great power competition into one argument about where the world is heading. Covering missile math, carrier vulnerability, demographic collapse, the Belt and Road as strategic colonization, and the technologies that could solve every crisis on the horizon, this is the book that ties everything else into one coherent warning. And one earned, hard-won optimism.

The Enshittification of America: How Private Equity Destroyed the Things We Love

A documented investigation into how private equity firms systematically acquired beloved American institutions, loaded them with debt, stripped out everything that made them worth visiting, and walked away wealthy while leaving communities with hollow shells of what they once had. Airlines. Restaurants. Department stores. Newspapers. Hospitals. Pharmacies. This book names the firms, documents the playbook, and makes the case that the degradation of American commerce was not inevitable. It was deliberate.

The Emasculation of America: How Russia's Long War Against the American Male Is Destroying the Nation From Within

Beginning with a KGB defector's 1984 warning that nobody heeded, this book traces the deliberate Soviet and Russian strategy to defeat America not through military force but through cultural subversion. Seeding an ideology through universities, amplifying it through social media, delivering it through institutions that now enforce it as policy. Applying academic cult identification criteria to gender ideology, documenting the biological attack through endocrine disruption, and tracing China's acceleration of the same strategy through TikTok, this is not a culture war book. It is a national security argument.

The Villainization of America

America ended slavery, defeated fascism twice, rebuilt its enemies after defeating them, created the largest middle class in human history, and produced more medical and technological breakthroughs than any nation that ever existed. Somehow a significant portion of its own citizens have been convinced it is the primary source of evil in the world. This book documents how that happened, who executed it, and why the psychological campaign to make Americans ashamed of their own country is inseparable from the economic and cultural attacks documented in the two preceding volumes.

Watch the Other Hand: Politics as Cover for the Kleptocracy

While Americans argue about culture war flashpoints and election outcomes, a quieter operation has been moving wealth and power from public hands into private ones at a scale most citizens never see. The political theater is real and exhausting and often deeply felt. It is also doing work for the people whose interests would not survive a population paying attention to what was actually happening. This book documents the kleptocratic capture happening behind the visible politics, names the mechanisms, and traces how the visible politics functions to keep attention pointed elsewhere.

Manufactured Fear: How Crisis Becomes Profit

Every era has its emergencies. The current era has manufactured ones, engineered to maintain a state of generalized anxiety that benefits specific industries and political coalitions. The fear is not invented. The proportions are. This book traces how a healthy capacity for legitimate concern was converted into a permanent state of alarm, names the actors who profit from it, and documents what happens to a population that lives at sustained emergency pitch for years on end.

The Death of Privacy: They Know Everything, You Know Nothing

The surveillance system that the citizens of free societies were promised would never be built has been built. Not by a single state with a single agenda but by a coalition of corporate platforms, advertising infrastructure, data brokers, and government agencies that share the substrate even when they do not coordinate the use. This book documents what is actually known about each individual user, who knows it, what they do with it, and what the absence of meaningful privacy means for political freedom in a society that depends on individuals being able to think and act without continuous monitoring.

The Wrong Fight: How the Climate Response Became the Climate Problem

The climate is changing, the consequences are real, and the response that was supposed to address them has been captured by interests that are using the response as a vehicle for their own purposes. The result is a policy regime that produces consequences which would be unacceptable on their own terms but become acceptable because the alternative is framed as denial. This book separates the science from the policy capture, names the specific failures of the current response, and argues for what an honest climate strategy would look like.

The Quiet War: How America's Adversaries Attack Without Firing a Shot

The hot wars of the twentieth century have been substantially replaced, against the United States in particular, by sustained operations that operate below the threshold of military response. Information operations. Cultural subversion. Economic coercion. Cyber penetration of critical infrastructure. Strategic drug supply campaigns. These are the instruments of the quiet war, and they have been working. This book documents the campaigns currently underway against the United States, names the state actors directing them, and explains why the inability to recognize them as warfare is itself one of the campaigns' objectives.

The Dumbing Down: How American Schools Stopped Teaching Children to Think

American schools have been progressively converted from places where children were taught to think into places where children are processed for credentials. The conversion was not an accident or a failure of execution. It was the predictable outcome of policy choices that prioritized measurable outputs over the difficult work of cognitive development, and that defined educational success in ways that did not require it. This book documents what was lost in the conversion, when the choices were made, and what would have to change to teach thinking again.

The Pattern: How the Enemies of You Work Together

The enemies named across this series are not parallel items on a list. They are a system. Cognitive erosion makes civic collapse possible. Civic collapse creates the conditions for kleptocratic capture. Kleptocratic capture funds the manufactured fear that legitimizes the surveillance state. The surveillance state runs on the educational system that produced citizens who cannot evaluate what is being done to them. Each enemy reinforces the others. None of them can be addressed in isolation. This book is the synthesis: how the system operates as a system, why the standard frame of fix-this-one-problem is itself part of the problem, and what counter-strategy looks like for someone who can finally see the whole shape of the attack.

The Debt Trap:* How the Financial System Was Designed to Extract From You*

Student loans that cannot be discharged in bankruptcy. Credit cards engineered to keep balances revolving. Mortgages structured so the first ten years of payments are mostly interest. Buy-now-pay-later services that have re-engineered impulse purchasing to operate on an installment basis. Auto loans that now run seven years and underwater within twelve months. Each financial product looks like a service. Each one is a specific design choice about who pays whom over time, and the design has consistently moved in the same direction. This book traces the architecture of consumer debt as a wealth extraction system, names the policies and corporate decisions that built it, and explains why the standard personal-responsibility framing is the cover story that lets the system continue.

The Sick Industry:* How American Medicine Profits From Keeping You Sick*

The American healthcare system spends more per capita than any other developed nation and produces worse outcomes on most measures that matter. The reason is structural. Chronic illness is more profitable than cure. Symptom management is more profitable than prevention. The food industry produces the conditions that the pharmaceutical industry then medicates. The hospital system bills by procedure, not by health. The medical research apparatus is funded primarily by entities with financial interests in particular conclusions. This book documents the architecture of medical extraction, names the specific incentive structures that produce it, and explains why the conversation about fixing healthcare has been confined to the question of who pays rather than what is being paid for.

The Gambling Machine: How America Made Predatory Gambling the Default

In 2018, sports betting was illegal in nearly every U.S. state. By 2024, it was legal and aggressively advertised in most of them. The expansion was not driven by public demand. It was driven by industry lobbying that succeeded because the public attention was on other issues. The new gambling environment is engineered with the full machinery of behavioral psychology: variable rewards, push notifications, free credits that require deposits, in-game betting that runs faster than judgment can keep up with. The financial outcomes are predictable and documented. The social outcomes are accumulating. This book traces how the legalization happened, who profited, and what is now being done to the people the new system has captured.

The Loneliness Engine: How American Life Was Structured to Isolate You

The third places where Americans used to encounter each other are gone. Bowling leagues, fraternal organizations, churches, neighborhood bars, civic clubs, parent-teacher associations: all measurably smaller, in many cases by orders of magnitude, than they were thirty years ago. The replacements are commercial products that provide the appearance of connection while delivering its opposite. This book documents the destruction of the institutions that made American social life functional, names the economic and policy forces that did the destroying, and traces the consequences for mental health, civic participation, and the basic human capacity to be known by other people.

The Theft of Childhood: How American Kids Stopped Becoming Adults

Children spend more time on screens than in any previous generation, less time outdoors than any previous generation, and reach standard milestones of independence later than any previous generation. The teen mental health collapse that accelerated after 2012 is not mysterious. The mechanism is documented. Phone-based childhood, helicopter parenting, the elimination of unsupervised play, the medicalization of normal developmental difficulty, and the school system's drift toward credentials over capacity have produced a generation that is anxious, fragile, and structurally unprepared for adulthood. This book names what was taken, who took it, and what would have to change for the next generation to get a different result.

Books by Richard Lowe

See books by Richard Lowe at

https://masterofworlds.com

Get free publishing insights and industry updates at

https://thewritingking.substack.com

For ghostwriting and book coaching services see

https://thewritingking.com

Index